OLD MEN
REMEMBER

———

OLD MEN REMEMBER

WILLIAM DOUGLAS HOME

COLLINS & BROWN

First published in Great Britain in 1991
by Collins & Brown Limited
Mercury House
195 Knightsbridge
London SW7 1RE

A CIP catalogue record for this book
is available from the British Library

ISBN 1 85585 002 0

Acknowledgements
The author and publishers are grateful to the Hulton
Picture company for permission to reproduce the copyright
photograph of Ralph Richardson

Typeset by Falcon Graphic Art Limited
Printed and bound in Great Britain by The Bath Press

LIST OF ILLUSTRATIONS

———

To Rachel, my children and
my grandchildren

CHAPTER 1

I have written three books to date, all of them autobiographical — the first taking me up to the end of World War Two, the second from then into the mid-1970s, and the third composed of letters written to my parents during wartime which, unknown to me, my mother had preserved.

Some might consider that to be enough.

Yet people often say to me at dinner, perhaps in self-defence, if and when they get the chance to comment after I have told them endless tales about my family and others, 'Why not write them down? Your memory's phenomenal, but one day you will be no longer with us — so why not write them down?'

So here I sit in my blue-chintz armchair, from which uphol-stered launching-pad some forty plays have taken off, while others still wait in their hangars patiently for a production, writing my fourth book.

So much by way of explanation. Beyond that, I do not think that any apology is needed for a fourth volume when one considers the volumes written on themselves and others by a host of scribblers such as (to mention only two) James Agate, the dramatic critic, who wrote six — or was it eight? — autobiogra-phies, or Brian Johnston, my old school friend and my youngest daughter's godfather, who has produced so many books in his time that his faithful readers find it hard to imagine how there can be enough jokes left in this sad world to fill another volume. Yet somehow he manages to track them down, never mind how old they are — indeed he much prefers them that way.

'Old jokes are the best,' he once said to me, more than once, in fact, 'as are old memories — the reason being that, as is the case with vintage port, they have matured with age.' Not that I intend to recount jokes except in passing. My intention, rather, is to write about myself a great deal less than in the past, and to concentrate instead on memories of family and friends which have come back to me since my last book was published. That said, I thought that my readers might find it helpful if I sketched in some of my own as well as my family background. Naturally I felt somewhat nervous at the prospect of repeating myself. But my publisher assures me that this does not matter, pointing out that readers who have read those early works — the first of which was published back in 1954 — are likely to be few and far between and would, in any case, have long ago forgotten the experience.

Born in Edinburgh in 1912, in Randolph Crescent, where my son was born forty years later, I returned to Springhill, Coldstream, Berwickshire the moment that my mother was deemed fit enough to travel. Here I spent the first few years of my life, looking out across the Tweed towards the Cheviot Hills. Later, at the end of the Great War, my father having returned from Gallipoli and then from Ireland in one piece, we moved to Hirsel, four or five miles down the Coldstream road, on the death of my grandfather.

In those days the Hirsel shared with Douglas Castle in Lanarkshire, some seventy miles to the west, the title of the Family Seat. Now the latter is no longer there, having been pulled down when a coal seam was found under it. Part of Hirsel House was standing at the time of Flodden, while Douglas Castle was built on the site of an early building known to Sir Walter Scott as Castle Dangerous, one tower of which still survives. Hirsel, if my estimate is correct, has but 2,000 acres whilst Douglas boasts more than 30,000 acres. Staff employed in those days — headed by a housekeeper and a butler, parlour maid and odd man and a flock of housemaids — were transportable from one house to the other when the family migrated. Most of the year was spent at Hirsel, with the summer (or grouse-shooting) months at Douglas. And until I went to school, this was the pattern of my life.

My first instructor was my mother, at whose knee I learned the rudiments of good behaviour and the basic facts of Christianity. From her, I passed into the schoolroom, where my sister Rachel was already installed, and came under the tuition of Miss Pattenden from Purley, who had taught my elder brothers, Alec and Henry, and my elder sister, Bridget. Whether she suspected that one of her pupils would one day become Prime Minister, I am in no position to assess. I only know that she gave of her best and taught the members of a large and varied family of children with both patience and forbearance.

Schoolroom holidays for Rachel and myself began when our two elder brothers came home. The spring holiday was spent at Hirsel, with me sitting in the back of a boat watching my father fishing in the Tweed and almost always catching something with a sixteen-foot rod. This was followed by an after-tea trip down to the Leet which meanders through the valley below the house. Here I would observe my father dropping a fly above some rising trout, and often catching one.

The summer holidays at Douglas I spent in my father's grouse-butt, keeping out of the way of his loader and indeed himself and trying, largely unsuccessfully, to keep an eye out for the birds as they approached over the high top of the butt. Only in the final seconds would I catch a glimpse of them as they flew by, and hear the whirring of their wings, the flapping of the flankers' flags, and the banging of the guns to right and left. Then, when the final whistle had been blown by Mr Telfer, the head keeper, I would scramble out to pick my father's birds up, if they had not already been gathered by the dogs from the butts next to him.

Evenings were spent in the woods along the Douglas valley, treading in my father's footsteps, looking for a roe-buck. He never used to shoot them, though in later years he taught me how to stalk them or to lie in wait for them on some enchanted evening on some heathery slope, far above the smoke-stacks of the coalmines up and down the valley.

Winter holidays were spent at Hirsel for the pheasant-shooting, standing to the right-rear of my father — which he taught me was the only safe place for a hanger-on to stand — and watching him bring down the pheasants or, on red-letter days, the woodcock up at Bonkyl on the way to Grantshouse. The woodcocks came there in substantial numbers for the winter from their breeding-grounds in Northern Europe: so insistent is their instinct for migration that — according to my father and my brother Henry — lighthouse-keepers on the west coasts of these islands have sometimes seen large flocks fly past at night, heading out to sea towards what must inevitably be a mass grave.

When I got into my teens, I graduated to a .22 rifle and a trout rod of my own. The former I would discharge hopefully at rabbits feeding on a hill called Hirsel Law and in the valley down which the Leet ran — the latter I would flog the Leet with, in the hope that some unwary trout would hazard a bite of my badly-tied-on fly. Later on, when I grew more mature, a sixteen-bore gun superseded the small rifle, while a salmon rod replaced the trout rod when I graduated to the Tweed.

When I was about fourteen, I remember the first (and almost certainly the last!) two-pound trout I ever caught, on the River Leet. One evening I had crossed the Ladies Bridge and turned left up towards Dunglass Bridge, when I saw a circle on the surface, denoting a rise, cast my fly upon the waters and hooked a Leviathan after which I hurried home to show my catch to any of the family who cared to look at it.

Years later I caught a ten-pound salmon from the bank of the Tweed just below Springhill. This stream is seldom fished for salmon, because it hardly ever holds any, but I always liked to try it nonetheless. I was staying with my mother (and my sister Bridget) at Springhill (then the dower house to the Hirsel) to which she had returned in her widowhood, and knowing that Alec was fishing the beat that day from a boat, I rang up the Hirsel to find out if he would object to my fishing from the bank that evening.

'Not a bit,' he said. 'But you won't catch one.'

'Never mind,' I told him, 'I'd like to have a go.'

'Well, try by all means,' he replied.

I rang him back that evening before dinner to inform him that I had just landed a ten-pounder.

'That's extraordinary,' he said, 'I tried it all the afternoon myself and never got a touch.' Who but a fisherman would tell so weak a story!

After my initial education at my mother's knee, via Miss Pattenden, I made my first trip to London when I went to Berwick Station with my father en route for King's Cross and Ludgrove School. In those days, in the early Twenties, Ludgrove was situated at New Barnet in Herts, but just before World War Two it was moved to the outskirts of Wokingham. Nearly seventy years later (in 1990) Prince William enrolled as a pupil at Ludgrove. This I mention not for snobbish reasons (though my children will not let me get away with that denial) but because his first term there prompted an amusing headline in the *Daily Mail*. 'Lady Di will be relieved to learn this' it read — before going on to quote from an article in a local newspaper in Wokingham which ended with the memorable phrase 'Capital punishment was abolished four years ago at Ludgrove.'

We sent our son Jamie to Ludgrove in the early Sixties and, if I may speak for him, he enjoyed his time there. We enjoyed our visits to him, too. The joint headmasters, Alan Barber and Tim Shaw, were a friendly pair, and after Tim retired he lived near Goodwood with his second wife. We often used to meet at Goodwood races. I once asked him, as we watched the horses walking round the paddock, whether he had been addicted to the sport during his teaching days.

'Of course, he answered. 'Why do you think schoolmasters have high-topped desks?'

Tim told me that on one occasion a small boy arrived at Ludgrove for his first term in a Rolls-Royce. His parents got out to greet the two headmasters, who were standing on the drive awaiting their new intake. After a short conversation, the father turned back to the car to fetch his son, remarking as he went that Tom (or Dick or Harry) could not wait to start his school life. He then tried the door, only to find it locked, after which the boy dropped the window slightly and told his father that he would not let him in unless he promised to take him home. The father called his wife to his assistance. She, too, failed to influence her son. So they shook hands with the two headmasters and drove their strong-minded offspring home again.

Next day, the car reappeared, and this time the boy accompanied his parents when they got out. Whether he had been cajoled or bribed or merely changed his mind remains a mystery.

As detailed on the board at Ludgrove, the new boys in my term, were Browne, Wellesley, Gilliat and Douglas Home. Browne's Christian name was Ulick. He later became Lord Oranmore and Browne, and later still he married somebody called Mrs Meyrick of night-club fame, who was a lady a lot older than himself. Since then I have not heard of him, though I rather fear that he may have left us.

Wellesley, now the Duke of Wellington (name-dropping again!), seems to have been a few years younger than the rest of us, judging by his annual birthday records in *The Times*. I intend to check the matter with him one day since this puts him about five years old when he turned up at Ludgrove, the rest of us being eight or nine.

Gilliat, the one I saw most of, has spent a large part of his life as the dedicated right-hand man to the Queen Mother and is still the friendly cheerful fellow that he was in our first term. Mrs Henley, the wife of one of the headmasters wrote to my Mama the day after I got there saying that 'I watched William talking hard to the boy next to him at breakfast.'

The two joint headmasters were a splendid couple, kindly dedicated and athletic. Mr Oakley had played football for his country, while Mr Henley was a cricketer of note.

Assistant masters, for the most part, were chock-full of character. The Bug (or Mr Stanborough) was the friendliest. He always came to my assistance when there was a 'Home bait', with my persecutors shouting 'codfish' at me (which was my pet-name at Ludgrove), calming me down with tact and understanding by describing some fictitious bird that he had just seen in the garden.

Bunco Brown was thoroughly austere, though rumour had it that he too had played rugger for his country in his youth. He wore a drooping moustache, whereas Mr Blore (otherwise known as Billy Bluff or, in line with his initials, Waste Paper Basket) was clean-shaven. He had written the school song, the first lines of which ran as follows:

> ''Tis the end of the term
> And we all must affirm
> That we're longing for home and its leisure
> But we'll ever be true
> To the flag — white and blue
> And the fair fame of Ludgrove we'll treasure
> Play up for Ludgrove
> Cheer cheer for Ludgrove
> For we'll ever be true
> To the flag white and blue
> And the fair fame of Ludgrove we'll tre-a-s-u-r-e.'

Eton came next where I made more friends, initially with Penrose Tennyson, a grandson of the poet, who persuaded me to write an article or two in a school magazine, and a young Scotsman from St Andrews called Jo Grimond, both of whom were in my house. The circle then widened to embrace contemporaries in other houses such as Tony Allen, Jimmy Whatman, Brian Johnston and Jimmy Lane Fox, to name but a handful.

All of these are with us still except for Jimmy Lane Fox, who died recently. He was Brian Johnston's greatest friend at school and in the army and thereafter — a good-looking and delightful fellow who became a house agent after the war. The firm in which he worked was called *Curtis and Henson* and Cecil Fielden, whose mother was my wife Rachel's great-aunt, was one of the partners.

Jimmy told me once that Cecil went into his office and sat down behind his desk one morning to open his mail and put his foot on some strange object. Without showing any sign of panic he picked up his telephone and dialled 999, after which he gave his name and address and reported that there was a burglar hiding underneath his desk. He then hung up and went on opening his mail until the police came and removed the frightened intruder, whom he had been using as a mat.

I hadn't been long at Eton, before I wrote my first play — a short piece in verse about the murder of a housemaster in pupil room — a room in which the housemaster instructed his boys in the evening.

The leading role was played by the Headmaster's son, Giles Alington, the brother of my sister-in-law, Alec's wife Elizabeth, who died — alas — in 1990. Rachel and I went to her memorial service at Westminster Abbey, arriving with one minute to spare after spending some time in a traffic jam near Guildford.

David, Alec's son, and Caroline, his eldest daughter, read the lessons admirably, while Lord Charteris gave the address which was outstanding for its understanding of a very special lady. Seldom, he implied, has any man been quite so lucky in his wife (and life) as Alec. He gave examples of her delightful sense of humour: such as when she remarked to some enquiring journalist that 'Considering the number of different names I've had in my life, it's surprising how infrequently I've been married!' Her tally amounted to five names in all — Alington, Lady Dunglass, the Countess of Home, Lady Douglas Home and Lady Home of the Hirsel.

He went on to say how she had nursed her absent-minded

consort on his trips abroad as Foreign Secretary, whispering 'Moscow' in his ear in case he should assume that he had just arrived in Washington or Peking or Rome. Her husband sometimes failed to study their travel schedule since on the plane he much preferred to read the racing form book which he always carried with him.

She was a sporting, understanding lady and an adept welder of the strongest family ties — quite a Herculean task when one considers the large number of eccentric relatives she had to deal with.

She always viewed the give-and-take of politics with a good deal of amusement. One evening, in the early days of Alec's career, she was sitting knitting in the car outside a village hall in which he was about to make a speech to his constituents in South Lanark. Her absence from the hall was due to the fact that she had already heard the speech two or three times that evening.

A miner who was wearing a smart suit and was on his way to the meeting met another miner, still covered in coal-dust, on the pavement by the car.

'And why're you no' going to the meeting?' he enquired of his friend. 'Because', said his friend, 'I've been a Tory now for forty years or mair and I'm just thinking that long-haired young fellow in there might put me off!' And he went on his way, while the young fellow's wife continued with her knitting, smiling to herself.

Smiling was one of her most charming habits — one that she shared with her mother, Hester Alington, a comfortable figure in my schoolboy days and a good friend and correspondent during the War, in which Patrick, her enchanting younger son, was killed.

'My poor wife' was how her husband, Dr Alington, invariably described her when speaking of her with affection. She charmed every schoolboy of whatever age who came to breakfast, lunch or tea in the Headmaster's house, which helped tremendously to put them at their ease in the erudite company of the Headmaster.

I recollect one breakfast there when I was very young and both my parents were week-end guests. I struggled to make conversation over the porridge, but it was not until my father dropped the teapot, cascading scalding tea-leaves over Mrs Alington's foot, that I felt at ease. All the attention was diverted away from myself, with my mother scolding her poor Charlie for his clumsiness and Dr Alington enquiring of his 'poor wife' whether she required a doctor (other than himself), which kind suggestion she laughed off as she limped over to the bell.

Another boy in my house who, like Jo Grimond went into politics, was Charles Mott Radclyffe, whose career began in 1942 when he stood as the (Tory) Coalition candidate in Windsor in a by-election. I opposed him, having fought an election in Scotland earlier that same year as an Independent, losing only by a margin of 2,700 votes — an honourable defeat considering that the might of Winston Churchill and his Coalition Government was ranged against me and my war-cry was a call for peace aims.

Charlie was supported by such political enemies of mine as Jim Thomas, a good friend of Alec's and a member of the Coalition Government as well as being a Conservative MP. One hot summer evening I was standing on the fringes of a meeting that Jim Thomas was addressing, en route to a meeting of my own. After he had finished his speech in support of my opponent, in which he deplored the intervention of an Independent in the middle of a war, and his chairman had declared the meeting closed, Jim came over to me where I stood in my lieutenant's uniform, warmly shook my hand and asked after my brother Alec, who was lying in a plaster-cast at Springhill with tuberculosis of the spine.

I told him I had seen him on my last leave and had found him cheerful and employing himself reading every history or biography that he could lay his hands on. Jim expressed his pleasure at the good news, smiled benignly, shook my hand again and then went off to his next meeting, leaving a bewildered crowd remarking on the friendship he had just shown towards the young man whose intervention he had been deploring a few minutes earlier — a fine example of the way in which a democratic politician should conduct himself.

Returning to my Eton friends, the closest, even though I was a lousy cricketer, was Tony Allen, who captained the Eleven. He went off to Cambridge when our school days ended whereas I went to Oxford, so I did not see a lot of him thereafter. Another friend was Clive Graham, now no longer with us, who was racing correspondent of the *Daily Express* after the War. I deliberately bring that up because it provides an excuse to tell the story of an article he wrote once after Cheltenham had been abandoned because of snow. Being a versatile sort of man, he decided to amuse his readers by describing a game of bridge he had played in Cairo in the War.

He and a fellow British officer were playing against two Australians, both pilots, who had evidently had a lot to drink that evening, resulting in a bid from one of them of Eight No Trumps.

Clive remonstrated with the bidder, telling him that Seven No Trumps was the maximum that he could make. This irritated his opponent, who picked up an empty bottle and began to wave it round his head.

Clive, being nothing if not sensible, said, 'All right, play it,' at which his opponent calmed down. During the hand, Clive's partner revoked, thus presenting the Australians, who made Six No Trumps, with two penalty tricks, which brought the score up to Eight No Trumps. History does not relate what happened after that. But one assumes that harmony reigned, whether or not any money passed from hand to hand.

When I arrived at Oxford, I continued to be friends with various cronies who had come from Eton with me such as Brian Johnston, the twins Hopetoun and Hope, Charles Wood and George Mercer Nairne, with the last four of whom I shared a house in Merton Street, outside which I left a hired car one night without its sidelights on. As a result, I lost my driving licence for one year, so I hired a horse and carriage and appointed Brian Johnston, who resided in another lodging house nearby, as my groom. He donned a sawn-off top hat with straw round it, tied string round his trousers just above the knee and held the horse and carriage for me while I was at lectures which he should have been attending himself.

I got sent down twice — once for climbing into college, and once for going off to London to a dance with George and leaving my bed vacant, which delinquency my landlady soon spotted and reported to New College. The Dean sent for me and I told him that Charles Wood could vouch for the fact that I had been in bed on the night in question, as he had come up to say goodnight to me and spent some time chatting to me. In fact this had made my landlady suspicious in the first place, but I did not tell him that. He said that, regretfully, he could not accept my story, and was going to send me to the Proctors. Off I went, and after they had charged me, I repeated my tale to them.

'In that case,' a Proctor said at once, 'we will ask Mr Wood to come round to confirm your story.' As he spoke he lifted up his telephone.

During the time it took Charles to get round to the Proctors' office, I began to worry not about him, but about his father, Lord Halifax, who was the Chancellor of the University. 'It won't do,' I told myself, 'to get Charles into trouble with his father.' So when he appeared, I informed the Proctor that I had been lying from the start.

After a short and whispered conversation, the Proctors announced that I would be sent down for the rest of the term. Then, after thanking Charles for coming round, they raised their mortar-boards and showed us from the room.

I came back the next term, and after one more year I finished my career at Oxford with a fourth-class Honours degree — given, according to one of those who examined me, for giving good answers to questions that had not been asked.

Fourth-class Honours degrees were done away with many years ago, and I consider myself lucky to have been awarded one. One other recipient I knew was Bouffy Gore, later Lord Arran, who got his a year or two before I got my own.

I do not think my friend George Mercer Nairne, now Lord Lansdowne (how these peers beset me!), landed a degree at all, although Hopetoun and Hope and Wood, all from the lodging-house in Merton Street, got through, though at what level I cannot be sure.

At the conclusion of my formal education, I went off on my first trip abroad with George in his new Humber car. We travelled via France to Spain, where our first night was spent in a monastery near Burgos. We were welcomed by the monks as *bona fide* travellers, and dined with the brethren in silence while one of them read aloud throughout the meal. That night I was frozen more or less stiff in the cell in which I slept — so much so that I put on all my clothes to keep warm in the middle of the night, then took my breakfast with the monks, again in silence, with the ends of my pyjamas sticking out from below my trouser turn-ups.

Another trip I took with George was to Italy, where George, who is and always was an art enthusiast, took me to a good many picture galleries. Although I was unfamiliar with most of the great artists and their pictures (with the possible exception of 'The Monarch of the Glen') George taught me quite a lot about art in the Prado or the Pitti or whatever foreign gallery you care to name. He paid me a great compliment the other day when he reminded me that I was very keen on Greuze, and always complained that his pictures were invariably hung above the door. He tells me that, on his more recent visits, he has noticed that the Greuzes have been moved to central positions on the main walls in most galleries. So much for my artistic sensibility in those days!

Having nurtured theatrical ambitions ever since I wrote my play at Eton, I began to work, first at RADA, then on stage in repertory, and then in the West End until the War broke out.

In between times, and while waiting for my call-up papers, I wrote two plays, the first of which, *Passing By*, was put on at the Q Theatre in 1940 while the second, written early that same year, was never produced at all. I also joined the Fire Service for three months: although we were never troubled by night raids at that stage of the War, I spent many nights in garages behind Cadogan Square until my call-up papers came through.

These ordered me to go to Maidenhead and report to an army camp just across the river from Cliveden. I became a private in the Buffs (and quite a drunken one at that, around the pubs in Maidenhead) — which regiment I stayed in, with a break at Sandhurst as an officer-cadet, until, just over four years later, I arrived, stripped of my rank, in Wormwood Scrubs.

But more of that hereafter. Meanwhile here endeth the chapter on my early life, so far as it concerns myself, my schooling and the start of my theatrical career.

CHAPTER 2

M y father was a small red-haired man with a friendly smile and a very loud voice. In the country he wore knickerbockers and a cap, while in Edinburgh or London he rested beneath a bowler hat. He came to London when he had to, such as when he was required to entertain his five sons on their mid-term holidays from school. This kept him busy for almost forty years!

He also took a house in Cadogan Square for the coming-out of his two daughters. He used to walk me up from there to Bond Street almost daily when I was a small boy and my sister Bridget was in the coming-out stakes — though why I happened to be staying there I cannot now recall. Perhaps I was on sick-leave from my private school after a bout of croup or something of that kind. The object of these expeditions was to visit a picture gallery devoted to the work of Thorburn (Archibald, the bird painter). This helped my father to get through the days between the dances — which he had to go to almost nightly, much to his distaste.

The fact was that he lacked rapport with London, even though he tried to get himself acclimatized as best he could by putting on the afore-mentioned bowler-hat, which he also wore to church in Coldstream or to Edinburgh on Tuesdays for the meeting of the British Linen Bank of which he was the chairman. This has never ceased to amaze me, since of all the men I ever met he always seemed the least well-tuned in to financial matters, with the possible exceptions of Lord Airlie, who was his successor, and his eldest son (my father's, not Lord Airlie's), both of whom struck me — and the latter strikes me still — as being almost wholly insulated from so worldly a diversion as finance.

Another thing that should surprise me — though it never did — is that he never once took me to see the House of Lords during all the time I knew him. I suspect his lack of interest was not because of any disrespect towards that institution, but because he did not see himself in the role of a debater. And I imagine he thought that the problems that beset his native land were not, perhaps, best dealt with in the House of Lords but on the spot and, in so far as they concerned him, in his capacity as lord lieutenant of Berwickshire.

And so, as soon as he could safely do so without letting down his children, male or female, he would hurry back to Berwick in a sleeper, with his faithful consort in the next one, and resume the life that suited him best — looking after the estates that many of his forebears had successfully defended from marauding Percys and the like from England, and attending to the problems and requirements of his county. This he did with total application and devotion to the tasks in hand.

Otherwise, he gave his time to his large family. I was lucky in my share of it because, as the youngest of five children born before the First World War began, I was still the baby of the family when he came home in 1918 — and remained as such until my younger brothers, Edward and George, both born in the early Twenties, took my place in due course.

This meant that, for ten or twelve years, with my sisters, Bridget and Rachel, closer to my mother and my elder brothers, Alec and Henry, both at school, my father saw much more of me than of his other children. As a result I got to know him well, and since I was a shy and nervous little boy, I looked upon him as my best friend. I had no fear of him, and always found him understanding, instructive and amusing.

I particularly enjoyed the way he talked about his friends, and I was seldom disappointed when I met them. They included Walter Forbes, 'dear old fellow' — as my father always called him — who came shooting in the summer. He it was who, in his room in Brown's Hotel, took his Purdey out a day or two before the Twelfth of August to have a practice swing, at which a shot went through the ceiling — either he or his loader had forgotten to unload it at the end of the last season. He was enchanting to younger children like myself, adjuring us 'not to look at me in that tone of voice' — a phrase which always made me laugh uproariously.

Another friend my father talked about quite frequently was someone whom he described as 'dear old Haig'. I met this character out on a shooting lunch in 1921 or 1922 when I was nine or ten, and found it hard to envisage the quiet and charming man eating his sandwiches beside me on a rug commanding all the British troops in France a few years earlier.

My father, as was his invariable custom when in the company of soldiers or ex-soldiers like himself, brought up the subject of the War towards the end of lunch. I remember his remarking, not for the first time, that, judging by his experiences in the Gallipoli Campaign, mortally wounded soldiers had invariably faced death philosophically and calmly, with the possible exception of a few young footballers who felt angry and frustrated by the prospect of no further games to come.

I thought then, and I still think, that my father launched this somewhat naive theory on Lord Haig in order to provide him with a crumb of comfort should his conscience still be troubled by the casualties incurred in France when he was in command. So far as I remember the Field Marshal made no comment on the subject, probably because he shared my view about his friend's initial motivation and had no desire to complicate the issue further. Anyway, the afternoon passed pleasantly enough and, when I said goodbye to him, I found myself — and this is no exaggeration — feeling sorry for him when I thought of the responsibilities that had been thrust upon him by the politicians back at home. And, on the way home, I soon discovered that my father felt the same as I did when I heard him say, half to himself, 'Poor old Haig,' as he filled his pipe and lit it.

A friend from just across the river on the English side of the border, was 'dear old John' otherwise known as Captain Collingwood, whose portrait now adorns the outside of the Collingwood Arms in Cornhill — the village where he lived — as a pub-sign when the weather is fine. His ancestors lived in Cornhill House at the time of Flodden, but I don't recall my father ever asking him on which side they had fought — for Lord Surrey in his bath-chair, or on the same side as my ancestor Lord Home. The latter went home on the night before the battle, assuming that it would not take place till the morning, and then re-crossed the Tweed only to find the remnants of the Scottish army wading back across the ford at Coldstream, which, in order to facilitate his own return, he had kept open.

Another friend my father had was 'dear old Joe', who had once bought a horse called Master Robert for a few pounds, which a friend observed out hunting (old Joe up) and sought permission to prepare for the National, which it won two years later — ridden by the friend.

I sometimes used to meet dear old Joe — alias Lord Airlie — in the New Club in Edinburgh when my father took me there to lunch after a visit to the dentist. As we appeared in the hall, old Joe would come up to my father, pick him up, raise him to his own height (which was not a great deal taller) and then shout in a loud voice, 'Good morning, Charlie, how are you, you little rat?' 'I'll be much better when you've put me down,' my father would reply. With his feet on the carpet again, he would then introduce me to his friend.

Writing of the Edinburgh dentist that I used to visit puts me in mind of one of my favourite stories of the First World War. In 1914, as is well known, there took place a Christmas truce in the no-man's land between the British and the German trenches in France and, since it was early days yet, nobody was punished for this fraternizing. But by Christmas 1915 discipline had been much tightened up by both the British and the German High Commands. In consequence what little fraternizing there was tended to be dropped on heavily.

Among those affected was a young guardsman called Ian Colquhoun, who had seen fit to hold a Christmas party with the Germans opposite his section of the line. This led to a court-martial being ordered by Lord Cavan, the overall commander of the area in which the fraternizing took place. What the outcome would have been had the court-martial taken place it is impossible to say. But a telegram from the King to Lord Cavan, reading 'Don't shoot my best officer', made sure that it did not. The reason why Sir Ian was the King's best officer has never been disclosed to me. Perhaps His Majesty employed the adjective to emphasize his point.

One day, after peace had returned, Lady Colquhoun, Sir Ian's faithful wife, who nursed a grudge against Lord Cavan for attempting to court-martial her beloved husband, took her children (one of whom is Lady Arran, the intrepid motor-boater) off to Edinburgh to see the dentist. When they came out, there before them in Princes Street, at the foot of the dentist's steps, was a limousine with Field Marshal Lord Cavan in full uniform and Lady Cavan in the back seat.

'Spit at that car, children,' ordered Lady Colquhoun, so the story goes, but history does not tell us — nor does Lady Arran — whether mother's order was obeyed or not. What it does tell us, though, is how profoundly loyal Lady Colquhoun was to her brave husband. I use that word advisedly, because another of his foibles, quite apart from fraternizing with the enemy, was to keep a young lion in his dug-out in the front line to keep the Germans out (although the story goes that it kept him out as well).

As for Lord Cavan, whose attempt to do his duty had been thwarted by his monarch, he was even smaller than my father: it is said (though this is not confirmed by my dear friend, his daughter, Elizabeth Longman) that when he was a small boy at Eton he could walk beneath the bar that spans a gap in the wall outside College Chapel with his top-hat on. As a footnote, it is worth remarking that his nickname all through his life was Fatty, though his name was Rudolph.

Both Sir Ian and Lord Cavan were known to my father, which I like to think excuses the recounting of the tale I have just told. And he, of course, admired them both — Sir Ian for his individual approach to discipline, and Fatty Cavan for attempting to uphold it.

Some might argue that this looks as though my father liked to have things both ways. Nothing could be further from the truth. It merely means that he respected every point of view and heartily applauded the emergence, as in this case, of a compromise — for engineering which, of course, the King also deserved to be congratulated.

While on the subject of kings, my father's attitude to royalty was one of deep respect. This led him to stand up, however deeply he might be involved in *The Times* crossword, every time the wireless played 'God Save the King'. Not only that: he made his family stand up as well, including his wife, even though she sometimes registered her independence by continuing to knit.

'We ought to give the little girl a present as I'm the lord lieutenant,' I recall him saying to my mother when Princess

Elizabeth became engaged, pointing at a cabinet in which there was a tray of knick-knacks.

'Don't you fiddle about with that,' said my mother as she came across the room and opened it. After a brief inspection, she removed a snuff-box. 'This'll do,' she said.

My father looked at it and said, 'It's got a crack across the lid, Lil.' 'Yes, I know,' my mother said, 'but she can put some plaster on it.'

Off it went — and who will ever know whether 'she' did or not!

That story might lead some to assume that my mother leaned towards republicanism. Not at all. She was a Lambton, that's all, with an independent mind and not a trace of anti-royalism. Possibly, she tended to believe that all men should be equal and that even though there might be some who were not, they should nonetheless be treated like the rest.

Although he respected royalty, my father called George VI 'the little king'. He stopped short of describing him as a 'poor little devil': that description he reserved for those who could not help themselves, like Hitler or Haile Selassie. I have told elsewhere of how he called the former 'a poor little devil' after seeing a picture of him in a Sunday paper marching between two field marshals. 'Look at that,' he said. 'Poor little devil! With his Sam Browne over the wrong shoulder and those fellows too afraid to tell him so.' In fact he loved his fellow men regardless of their shortcomings.

Now I look back on it, he may have been a little like Lord Longford, although not nearly so all-embracing in his charity. He had no snobbishness and, having been brought up by a host of servants, was friendly with them all and treated them as equals in theory, though not perhaps always in practice. As, for instance, when my mother said to him one morning, apropos the butler, 'Collingwood has just asked for a day off each week.'

'What for?' my father asked. 'He'll only go down to his house. And why the devil should he want to do that?' In fact, the house at the bottom of the lawn contained Mrs Collingwood, well worth a visit any day. But, even though my father knew this, he forgot that butlers, like the rest of us, require a bit of leisure

— rather more perhaps than he required himself. In spite of this, George Ernest got his day off thanks to his employer's wife.

When war broke out in 1939 the Collingwoods were staying with their son in Cumberland. Much to the amusement of our family, a telegram arrived which read 'Due to the outbreak of war, returning under cover of darkness by train'; and sure enough the Collingwoods arrived intact at Cornhill Station, to be greeted with much merriment by Jimmy Hall, my father's chaffeur. Jimmy was always much amused whenever my father forbade us to use his car for pigeon-shooting after he had been to Edinburgh for a meeting at his bank in the morning, on the grounds that it needed a rest. His eyes would twinkle, too, when we asked if he had been instructed to provide it with a bale of hay.

Apart from Mr Collingwood and Jimmy Hall and his brother Tommy, both chauffeurs, my favourites among the staff were the game-keepers at Douglas, led by Mr Telfer the head keeper, an outstanding man. The story goes that when my father let the moors at Douglas one year to an Indian prince, Mr Telfer found on the first day's shooting that he and his friends fell very far short of the safety standards, he regarded as essential; so, in the watches of the night, he and his two lieutenants, Messrs Carr and Bell, removed the shot from all the cartridges which had been laid out on the gunroom table ready for the next day.

When the guns returned to Douglas the next evening there was no bag but nor were there any human casualties, so Mr Telfer was well-satisfied. Not so the Indians, however, who had sworn at him throughout the day for allegedly driving the grouse over them in such a way as to make it extremely difficult to hit them. But this did not disconcert him either since my father, who deplored bad language, was not present — though on occasions, when some of brother Alec's shooting friends were in an adjacent butt, he had to listen to some very strong stuff even when the cartridges were quite correctly charged. As far as I remember, I never heard my father go beyond the word 'damn', and that very seldom. Nor did he like rude jokes or vulgarity of any kind.

When I was in my teens, I sometimes joined him over the port after dinner with some friend who had been with him in the army during the War. More often than

25

not, when the second or third glass of port had loosened up his guest's tongue, prompting him to tell some story decorated with distasteful adjectives, my father would get up and say, 'I think we ought to join the ladies as it's getting late, so let's finish it in there' — by which he meant the port and not the story. But of course, as he was well aware would be the case, his friend did neither.

Innuendoes and crude suggestions, even though made in jest, were anathema to him — as illustrated by his strong reaction to what my Uncle Claud (my mother's brother) once saw fit to write in an after-dinner game called Telegrams, which had been devised by, most probably, my brother Henry when there was no four for bridge.

Uncle Claud, always a cheeky fellow, had two other sisters. One of them, Violet Ellesmere, was — at least in my uncle's imagination — much admired by a Colonel Algy Trotter, who lived near Duns. There was nothing in it whatsoever, but it greatly amused my uncle to imagine his tall sister being wooed by the small colonel with a stammer from the next-door county.

He wrote out the following telegram, which he then read out aloud when his turn came: 'Violet Ellesmere, Merton, St Boswells, Roxburgh. Meet me Claridge's next Wednesday. Don't bother with a nightgown. Algy Trotter.'

Hardly had the last words left his lips than my father rose up from his chair, throwing down his crossword on the floor in a cold fury.

'Who wrote that disgusting thing?' he shouted.

Uncle Claud turned purple, but his courage, which had earned him a DSO in the First World War, did not desert him.

'I did, Charlie,' he said nervously.

'Then get out of the house,' my father said.

Silence fell for some time, interrupted only by strangled giggles from my mother and other members of the family. Then Uncle Claud got up, still purple, and left the room with Aunt Olive, who was also giggling.

Some of us followed them down to the hall to say goodnight, and Mr Collingwood came forward with their coats and scarves, suspecting something unusually dramatic must have taken place upstairs, though unaware of what exactly it had been until I told him about it later.

As Mr Collingwood opened the front door to let out my delinquent uncle and his wife, my father's voice rang out from the top of the stairs: 'You can come back, Claud, so long as you don't write a filthy thing like that again.'

So up the stairs we all trooped, leaving Mr Collingwood to shut the front door, and resumed the game in a more chastened mood — its progress interrupted at frequent intervals by sounds which suggested that Aunt Olive had not quite recovered from this devastating experience.

That was the only time I ever heard my father rebuke anybody seriously, so good-tempered and kind and benign was he. In a day or two, all was forgotten. Indeed, Telegrams was frequently enjoyed thereafter by his family and friends, though players were all told the story of our Uncle Claud's disgrace beforehand to discourage unsuitable flights of fancy during the evening's play.

Apart from that unique but minor episode concerning Uncle Claud, all our guests of whatever age were treated by my father with total friendliness and understanding — Alec's cricketing friends, Henry's point-to-point pals, my own school friends and my sisters' suitors were all persona grata with my father, though he sometimes said things in their presence which were nothing if not shrewd.

For instance, Jo Grimond came to stay and one evening, when Alec was discussing who should join which snipe-shooting party the next day, my father interrupted the discussion by remarking, 'Poor old Grimond doesn't want to go. He wants to stay at home and think.'

But poor old Grimond did go when the time came, though no doubt he spent a lot of time in thought while wading through the bogs. To this day, he sometimes recollects my father's tribute to his cerebral activity.

Nor were his comments on my girl-friends any less acute in later years. I asked a lovely girl once to come to stay for the Berwickshire and the Buccleuch hunt balls one January. In fact, she went to neither as she was not in the mood, but even so she stayed a week. The evening after she had left my father put his crossword down and remarked, 'Nice little girl, that Isobel Mills. Sat staring into the fire all the time she was here. Bad liver, I shouldn't wonder!'

Isobel, who recently died, alas, always conceded that his diagnosis could not have been more correct!

My Oxford friend, George Mercer Nairne, now Lord Lansdowne (pardon the name-dropping yet again), recently reminded me of the time when my father asked him if he would like to see some water-colours upstairs in the bedrooms. By then it was about half past ten at night, and the ladies had gone up to bed.

'Yes, very much indeed, Lord Home,' George said.

So up they went and looked at some very pleasant pictures in various rooms. Then my father said, 'There are some lovely Sanfords in here. Let's go in and have a look at them.' They went into a bedroom, turned on the light, and George saw some Sanfords hanging on the wall above the bed-head. Moving forward to the near-side of the bed, he raised his head to look at them.

'You'll see them better if you climb onto the bed,' my father said.

George did as he was bid and, as he did so, felt a movement up against the knee he had put on the bed, looked down and saw my mother, who had gone to bed at ten, just as she was opening her eyes.

'Oh, sorry, Lil, forgot you had turned in,' my father said, as he and George retreated. As they went downstairs, my father said, 'Come up in the morning after breakfast when the light'll be much better.'

After the Second World War my father was painted in his Thistle Robes by James Gunn. He did not much enjoy the sittings as they took him down to London. But he went through with them, making only one complaint. One night at dinner in Brown's Hotel he turned to my mother and said, 'What's that fellow's name who's painting me?'

'James Gunn,' she told him patiently.

'He's pinched my specs,' he told her, 'and I can't see what I'm eating.'

'Well, let's hope that he's not touching up your picture in yours,' said my mother. 'Get on with your fish.'

This reminds me of when my father and his son-in-law, my sister Rachel's husband Billy Scott, were on duty at Holyrood in Archer uniforms and plumed hats — or, to be more accurate, when Billy was on guard outside the palace while my father, during a short break, was treating himself to a cup of coffee and a bun in an adjacent marquee.

His thirst and hunger sated, my father went out to the marquee to find his son-in-law standing at full attention, waiting for the royal procession. Giving way to a kind thought he went back into the marquee, and secured another bun. He then marched over to his son-in-law and thrust it into his hand, leaving Billy with the choice of either dropping it or eating it. As far as I remember, in the interests of hygiene and tidiness, he chose the latter course, completing it just as the royal procession came in sight.

My father died in 1951. A few weeks earlier, John Henderson, the Coldstream doctor, had confided to me, as he got back into his car after a visit, that he did not think that he would last much longer.

Sure enough, he died the next month, just before my wedding, looking out across the valley to the River Leet that flowed beneath his drawing-room window.

Sad as I felt when I heard the news, yet even then I experienced a certain happiness from the belief that, however long I lived, the memory of an enchanting father would be with me always, undiminished by time. And now, forty years on, that belief has been most abundantly fulfilled: for invariably, in my waking hours each day, and often in my dreams at night, some memory of him comes back to me to cheer me on my way.

CHAPTER 3

My mother was slim and good-looking with dark hair and a good figure — taller than her husband, also less outgoing with a quiet voice and a gentle smile. She took a back seat when my father was alive, although her personality was no less strong than his. He ran the entertainment side of the family, so to speak, while she remained in charge of the administration, which she dealt with quietly and efficiently.

The story I told about Mr Collingwood in the last chapter illustrates who held the casting vote when it came to domestic matters.

She dealt with the delinquencies of her five sons and her two daughters sternly when occasion so demanded, yet with understanding when they were less blameworthy than at first appeared to be the case.

The nannies and the governesses she employed to tend and teach us in our early youth knew very well who ruled the roost and took care to observe the entirely fair rules that she imposed upon them.

Strange to say, she never sought to exploit her administrative talents in the Women's Institute or other such activities. Perhaps it was her shyness that prevented her from doing so — or perhaps the manifold and endless duties that her husband took on in such fields persuaded her that one at least of the two heads of the large family that she presided over ought to bear in mind that charity begins at home.

At any rate, her home was where she stayed for sixty years or more, except when she accompanied her 'silly little man', as she was wont to call him, down to London for her sons' week-ends off from school — which occurred far too frequently in her opinion, I imagine.

Apart from these thrice-yearly visits, plus her daughters' coming-outs referred to earlier — and, naturally, her honeymoon in 1903, spent down in England — I suspect she hardly spent a night away during her entire married life.

Mention of their honeymoon reminds me that, while changing trains in Edinburgh on the way home, Lil and Charlie, as they always used to call each other, took lunch in the Caledonian Hotel. Their maid, Miss Robertson, deposited the luggage in the entrance hall, then went off to have her own lunch elsewhere. When she returned the piece of luggage in which the Home family jewels had been packed had disappeared, nor was it ever seen again.

My father took this mishap philosophically, merely remarking that he hoped 'the poor little devil' who had stolen it would find its contents useful.

Nor was Lil unduly put out, it seems: she managed to get by, surviving throughout her marriage and thereafter on whatever rings, necklaces and occasional tiaras had been left at home.

She spent most of the First World War without my father, who was away in the army; bringing up her five children alone did not daunt her in the least, because her courage and self-confidence enabled her to ride out any storm.

Her courage was outstanding — so much so that she had all her teeth out in her later years without an anaesthetic, as she did not like the idea of the local 'jab' the dentist recommended to her. She returned in time for lunch entirely unmoved by her ordeal.

Only after, some weeks later, she had come back from Kelso with her new dentures in place was she in any way disturbed — they fell out onto the hearth just as she was shaking hands with a retired and somewhat nervous admiral my father had brought home to lunch after fishing.

Talking of hearths, one strange habit that my mother frequently indulged in during cold weather was to stand with her back to the fire, conversing with her guests, both male and female, while at the same time holding her skirt waist-high to warm her bloomers, as she always called them, and her stockings and her feet — by then she would have taken off her shoes as well and put them in the grate to warm.

I got to know her best after my father died, when she moved back to the first home she lived in after they got married — Springhill, which has since been sold.

Together with my eldest sister, Bridget, she lived on there into her eighties; the two of them were the sole residents, though a lady from the village came along to cook each day. On those occasions when she could not manage due to illness or some other cause, like holidays, my mother and my sister cheerfully stood in for her. And even when she was on duty, these two often did the washing-up, which my mother took to like a duck to water.

Visitors arrived continuously — the most frequent, since they lived in England, being her third son (myself), plus wife and children, who took up a lot of room. But we were always welcome and we mucked in to the best of our ability.

Apart from my own family, my brothers' and sisters' children and their friends all seemed to converge on Springhill at tea-time most days of the week during the Fifties, plus Uncle Claud (Aunt Olive had died earlier). As he got back into his car to re-cross the Tweed, Uncle Claud used to say, 'See you next week, if I'm not in my box by then.'

My mother led a quiet life in her old home, watching television to quite a late hour — a treat her husband would not have allowed had he still been around, as he always sent his Lil to bed at ten o'clock sharp — which is why George Landsowne had encountered her there while looking at the Sanfords.

She used to watch the boxing on the television with both hands over her eyes and a small slit between her fingers so that she could see the footwork only — she did not like to see the boxers hitting one another.

One more eccentricity I must record. When inspecting a baby she would hold over it a pair of scissors, the blades pointing downwards, and swing them gently to and fro above the baby's face. When the blades caught the light, the babies were much amused.

The thing that most endeared her to me was the way she wore her spectacles when they were not in use and especially when they were right on the end of her nose. Indeed, so much did this intrigue me that I sat down one day and drew a sketch of her — a thing that I had never done before (or since). I am convinced, although I was the artist, that it is as good a picture of her as it could be possible to draw and I am utterly delighted that the publishers have decided to put it on the back of this book's jacket.

Her eldest sister, Violet, used to come to tea at Springhill for a gossip from her home at Merton, further up the Tweed. Whenever we came in from playing with our children in the garden, my wife Rachel and I often found my mother and Aunt Violet — Bridget would be in the pantry hotting up the scones — both reading newspapers very intently. We felt sure that their gossip had been broken off when we came in, to be happily resumed when tea was over and we were out playing in the garden once again.

Aunt Violet lived on beyond ninety and, until she drew her last breath, every whiff of rumour she had read in the gossip columns was studiously sifted to discover whether there might be a grain of truth concealed in the hyperbole.

I vividly recall a visit to her home at Stetchworth, near Newmarket, when she was well over ninety. We went into her sitting-room but well before we could say, 'Hullo there, Aunt Violet,' she had called out to Rachel 'How true is it about Princess Margaret?' Whether Rachel knew or not, I can't remember. But what I can recall, years later, is the bright intelligence and twinkle in the eyes of her interrogator.

When my mother died, some years before Aunt Violet, Bridget occupied Springhill until she too died, having suffered from acute arthritis for some years. She was the second of the family and, like my father, she was almost a saint, having devoted all her life to looking after relatives who needed her assistance.

Of my mother's children, Alec was the eldest, followed by Bridget and Henry (known as the Birdman). Rachel came next, then myself, then Edward, now a farmer in the Borders, and finally George, who died in the War while on a training flight out of Vancouver Island.

All these I wrote about in my last book, since publication of which Bridget and Henry have departed this world. Nor is there much I can add to what I wrote about the survivors since they carry on as they have always carried on since I first met them — that's to say with a benign benignity.

Sir Alec, as I like to call him, although now aged

eighty-six or eighty-seven (I have no Debrett to check with) has changed not at all, still handing out the racing tips with satisfying regularity.

I do not think that this activity had started when I wrote my last book, so a word of explanation may be called for.

I had noticed for some years that he had tended to have good ideas about horses even when he was Prime Minister, so I wrote to him one day — when he had more or less retired from politics — suggesting that in future he should call me up whenever he had something he thought worth tipping. I added that, as a reward for a successful venture, I would pay him 10 per cent of any winnings that resulted from his deliberations.

I am happy to record that in the first year of our operation he rang me one Friday after breakfast during Ascot week and tipped me off about half-a-dozen horses.

Having won a modest sum the day before, I called my bookie up and said, 'What is a mix-up bet on half-a-dozen horses called?'

'A Heinz,' he told me.

'Right,' I said, concluding that meant fifty-seven bets in doubles, trebles, Yankees and Canadians etc. 'I'll have a one-pound win Heinz on the following six horses.'

I gave him the names of Sir Alec's tips, and set off to Ascot to see what transpired.

The first three won; the fourth, the favourite, went down by half a length or so; and then the fifth and sixth won also. I drove home to my beloved wife, elated yet, strange to say, still sober.

Around drinks time that same evening, I received a call from Arundel where Alec was staying the week-end. 'We've won £20,000 according to Lavinia,' he said.

'Lavinia must put on rather more than I do, in that case,' I told him. Nonetheless, his 10 per cent of what I won necessitated my writing out a cheque for £950.

I tell this rather vulgar story (as my mother would have called it) to bring cheer to any punter who has reached the stage in life where he (or she) believes that miracles no longer happen.

All this occurred some years back, since when we have suffered fluctuating fortunes. Nonetheless, I do not think that we have more than dented the reward that came to us on that memorable day, however hard we have tried.

To come right up to date, he gave me the Oaks winner last Saturday, and Ascot is not far ahead!

He had a stroke last year (in 1990). He was staying with us and my son-in-law, Harry Marriott, and I had walked him down to a farm beyond the village green to have a look at a pot-bellied Vietnamese pig belonging to Mr Warr, the local farmer. On the way home he was taken ill. I ran back for the car while Harry supported him until a kind couple brought a chair out of their cottage for him to sit on. He had another turn that night. Later it transpired that he had had two previous turns in Scotland but had kept them to himself because he didn't want to miss Elizabeth's memorial service in Westminster Abbey. Our village doctor, Ann Young, arranged for an ambulance to take him to a Winchester nursing home from where he returned to Scotland a few weeks later, since which date he has been getting better every day, apart from having trouble with his eyesight.

Writing of his wife, Elizabeth, who died in 1990, reminds me that I have not written half enough about her in my previous books, no doubt because I wrote too much about myself in those days. Let me make up for it now.

I met her first at Eton, where her father was Headmaster. He was an outstanding man of whom much has been written. His wife was a Lyttelton with all the charm associated with that family. They had six children — four girls and two boys — of whom three daughters still survive.

I was still up at Oxford and was dining one night with my New College mate, Brian Johnston, when I said to him, 'Good news today. Elizabeth and Alec are engaged.'

'Well, bless my soul,' he said, 'I was engaged to her myself last year at school.'

'Well, why didn't you marry her?' I asked.

'Because', he replied, 'we were in the rhododendrons together one Sunday morning and Dr Alington walked by in his surplice on his way to Chapel and said, "Come out of there, Elizabeth, you can do better than that."'

Of course, he heartily denies now that he ever said that, but my memory is not to be ignored.

Elizabeth stood by her Alec through a long and active life and gave him quite invaluable support.

Indeed, in my view — and, I think, in hers — he might have been prime minister for longer had he asked for her advice before resigning prematurely as Tory Leader after being defeated by Harold Wilson in the 1964 general election. Judging by the small number of seats the Conservatives lost in the general election, he might well have carried on as Leader and beaten Mr Wilson in the next one.

History — or rumour, anyway — records that he went home to tell his wife that he had given up when it was too late to reverse the situation. Nonetheless, he resurfaced later, and most usefully, as Foreign Secretary under Mr Heath, again with her support.

Henry was called the Birdman in a nature programme in which he took part in Scotland in the post-war years. He also wrote a book of that name. He was a great ornithologist and a keen shot (two traits which sometimes go together!). He was also an intrepid rider and bore many scars as evidence of that addiction. He was also fond of a drink — indeed, in his later years, the keen intelligence which had been his was drowned by his excessive alcoholic intake. However, he remained as kind and as prone to tell a good tale as he always had been — never mind how near the knuckle or how far from the truth it was!

Margaret Spencer, Henry's first wife, is now well over eighty, and still as fresh and as lively as when I first met her. She lives in Burnham Market where she organizes concerts, picture exhibitions and the like with unfailing zeal. She it was who wrote to my mother, when she was engaged to Henry, 'Henry's coming up on the night-train on Friday so that he can shoot on Saturday at Hirsel. I'll be coming up on Saturday on Dinah' — by which she meant the day-train to Edinburgh known as 'The Diner'.

Her first child was Robin, a delightful red-haired boy who combined piano-playing in such places as the Berkeley Hotel with daytime work at J. Walter Thompson. He was also a photographer of great ability.

When he was very young he fell in love with a Swedish princess called Bernadette. This earned him much publicity and sometimes, when we drove him down from London for the week-end, we would find it necessary to rush him to the car and put him on the floor so as to avoid the crowd of journalists eager for news about the progress of the romance. On one occasion, when Rachel and I arrived at his cottage for a meal, we found him talking on the telephone for an interminable period. We helped ourselves to drinks and had a game of croquet before he joined us.

'Who was that that you were talking to?' I asked him, thinking that I knew the answer full well.

'The old King of Sweden,' he said.

'The call must have cost the earth,' I told him.

'Never mind that,' he said, 'I reversed the charges.' After which he took aim at the first hoop.

Evidently his suit was not much appreciated by the lady's family. In fact, according to my spies, Sir Alec had a visit at the Foreign Office from a Swedish diplomat who more or less implied that Robin's breeding might not be quite up to the requirements of a Swedish princess, if she were to make a satisfactory match.

It is not recorded whether Alec raised the question as to whether a young female descended from one of Napoleon's marshals was quite up to the standard that he would have welcomed in the wife of his first nephew.

Anyway, the romance fizzled out and Robin married Sandra Paul — a model and a lady of great beauty: between them they produced a son called Sholto, who now works in advertising, just as his father did. Robin and Sandra parted some years after marriage — amicably but, alas, for ever. She is now the wife of Michael Howard, the politician.

Then, one dreadful day in 1964, Robin shot himself while in a state of deep depression. This was a most tragic blow to all his family and friends, because he had been greatly loved, not only for his charm, but also for his kindliness and friendliness to all and sundry.

Rumour had it — and I think it likely that it had some substance to it — that he had severe financial troubles, brought about by over-betting. Whether I am right or not,

I suspect that he may have tried to get back the money he had lost, not by sticking to the same-sized bet consistently and waiting for a change of luck, but by staking enough to wipe out any deficit, however large it may have been. To act thus is of course, a fatal error and invariably leads to disaster. Speaking as an operator on a very small scale, I have found that unshakeable determination not to vary the stake earns its own reward.

I hope that Uncle William's love of racing did not lead poor Robin astray in his youth: and if it did, I comfort myself with the thought that I discouraged him from ever betting too high. By the time of his tragic ending, he was on his own, and I had no idea that he had fallen victim on a large scale to the racing bug — which no doubt emanated from whatever Lambton blood flowed through him via his maternal grandmother. She, of course, was so strong-minded that she never felt a like temptation or, if she did, she never succumbed to it — unlike Robin, who, alas, was made of much less stern stuff.

There were ladies in his life as well towards the end, with some of whom things did not run too smoothly: his sensitivity was such that he could not face life or laugh at its misfortunes any longer.

We asked him to come and stay with us — he had a house near Pulborough at the time — but he said that he had too many dogs and did not want to cause us any inconvenience. We told him that did not matter, but he would not come. That was our last talk with him. Next week, on my way to Brighton to see my new play, *The Secretary Bird*, on its pre-West End tour, I thought to myself as I went through Petworth that I should perhaps go via Pulborough, even though it would take longer, and see Robin — but since I was late already, I thought it better not to.

Robin got his flair for music from his mother and the happiest memories I have of him are bound up with the many pilgrimages we made to the Berkeley Hotel, between 6 and 8p.m. to listen to him playing to a happy and appreciative audience. Both my parents came once, as I recollect, to listen proudly to their talented young grandson.

The tragic news broke in the week the new play came on in the West End. What a tragedy; what a waste of a most worthwhile life as well as of a most enchanting nephew.

His younger brother Charlie's life was tragic too, though this was not of his own making. He was taken ill while still the young Editor of *The Times* and died prematurely, leaving behind him his wife Jessica, and two young sons, Tara and Luke.

He was delightful — always friendly, always witty and as brave in his last illness as a man could be. He kept on working at his editorship to the end, thanks to Rupert Murdoch's trust and understanding. This helped him greatly since he had no time to brood — not that he ever brooded during all the happy years I knew him.

One can best describe him as a cheeky, friendly little fellow, who had been a Colleger at Eton and was an intrepid rider, like his father. After Eton, he was in the army for a while before going out to Kenya on Sir Evelyn Baring's staff. That task concluded, he returned to Britain and secured a job in Glasgow on the *Scottish Daily Express*, where, according to his story, he got his first scoop while sunbathing beside Loch Lomond after lunch one afternoon, when a commercial lorry left the road and settled down beside him on the water with its driver still in one piece.

He came down south in due course to become the Defence Correspondent of *The Times*. He crossed the Iron Curtain frequently in his quest for stories, and never failed to write outstanding articles on his return.

He would often call me up about my latest letter to *The Times* (a lifelong habit of mine). These always finished up on his desk, from which he transferred them into his waste-paper basket nine times out of ten — although, of course, he never would have thought of bypassing his Letters Editor.

He rang me once, dear fellow, when *The Times* was on strike to give me the name and number of a senior compiler of the crossword puzzle, suggesting that I ask him to send me one or two of his creations which had not been printed. I failed to take advantage of this very friendly offer, as I thought that the compiler would most likely want to keep them up his sleeve for use at some later date.

Although he had a most attractive brother in the shape of Robin he was never over-shadowed by him: his own personality was just as vibrant, with, perhaps, an aura of responsibility, which had either eluded Robin, or been eschewed by him.

Charlie had a most endearing approach to life. He was a very strong though quiet personality, with very definite views and at the same time an ever-present wish to help those whom he thought to be in need of it. In fact, he much resembled his grandfather — my own father — in being tolerant, understanding and invariably ready to hold out a helping hand.

I remember he stayed with Rachel and myself one week-end, meaning to return on Sunday night to London so as to resume work next day. But the three-handed bridge which we had played throughout the week-end caused him to change his plans. Because of his total involvement, he missed two Sunday evening trains on that Sunday evening, and all the trains from Petersfield on Monday. Finally, the bridge marathon concluded to his satisfaction, he allowed me to conduct him to the station early on Tuesday morning.

Warmth of character was a most noticeable trait of Charlie's from a very early age. I well remember being in my mother's drawing-room at Springhill one autumn evening just as it was getting dark: I was working on my crossword, my sister Bridget was knitting and my mother was reading in her armchair, while between us on the floor sat Charlie, then aged four or five, playing with his bricks. My mother shifted in her chair once or twice, trying to pick up the fading light on the page she was reading, at which Charlie got up from the floor, went over to the standard lamp beside my mother's chair, and switched it on. He then turned to his grandmother and said, 'Grannie, you are your own worst enemy,' and went back to his bricks.

As he sat down, his grandmother replied, 'You pompous little creature, get on with your bricks.' But I noticed that she had a smile on her face as she spoke — as had Charlie, when I looked down at him.

Henry had two more sons, George and Peregrine, by his second wife who was Norwegian, and a third wife, Felicity, a South African. Now he is gone, one misses him acutely for his charm, his outspokenness and his all embracing love for birds.

'Why sit here,' I once asked him on holiday on the Ile de Ré, off La Rochelle, in France, 'looking at all those very ordinary sparrows when the island's full of Great White Herons that I want to photograph?'

'You bloody fool,' he told me, 'they're not ordinary sparrows. They're Spanish sparrows.'

God rest his enchanting soul!

William (myself) was the next son, and married a lady with a name that differs from my own — but more of that anon. We have four children: Jamie, Sarah, Gian and Dinah.

Jamie, married to Christine, a daughter of the trainer, Willy Stephenson (who won the National with Oxo and the Derby with Airborne), has one daughter, Emily, who is a splendid child. At lunch one day she left her chair, walked round the table to her father, took his plate away and said, 'What would you like to eat now, my dear friend?' She calls me 'rag-bag' for some reason best known to herself, a nickname I accept with equanimity. Jamie was a race-horse trainer with a list of quite impressive races to his credit, but he gave it up because he had a shortage of Sheiks in his stable. Now, like his old father, he is looking for a job.

Sarah, our eldest daughter, married to Nick Dent, a steady, restful fellow and a skilful sailor with an ocean-going fishing boat, has one son and two daughters (plus another son, born last week April 1991). Rosemary, the eldest, is both sound and sensible with logical and very definite views.

'Felix can't be a frog, Grandpa,' she says, when I use my nickname for her little brother, 'and I'll tell you why — because frogs don't wear trousers. And he does,' which serves to put me in my place.

Her sister, Catherine, is more outspoken than is Rosie when it comes to criticism, telling Grandpa not to talk a lot of nonsense in uncompromising terms. Once when told by her mother to sit down and write to thank her Grandparents for presents — a task Rosie was fulfilling at the time — she said, 'I'm sorry, Mummy, but I'm going to arse around today if you don't mind.'

The Frog, himself, has definite opinions, like his elder sisters. For example, when told by his mother that he was to be a page at his Aunt Dinah's wedding he replied, 'I'm not. I won't be turned into a page in a book.'

And he stuck to his decision when — though fitted out in his silk shirt and knee breeches — he would not function in the church, although at the reception he enjoyed himself immensely. Only recently, he said to me at lunch, 'You are a very messy eater, Grandpa,' which can only indicate that he is on the ball.

Gian, our unmarried daughter, is a favourite among all the grandchildren and has been looking after Sarah since the fourth child was born.

Gian is an eccentric girl with lots of charm and she is also a hard worker in her role of literary editor, although her working hours seem to her aged father to be not so regular as his. Irregularity would seem to suit her well, however. She has a long-standing friend called Tahar Hey Dada who is a Berber and an architect with quite a flush of letters after his name. Though I do not always understand each word he says, I find him charming and a worthy rival on the croquet lawn, a game that he has taken up with great enthusiasm.

Dinah's husband, Harry Marriott, deserves a mention since, like the four grandchildren, he did not feature when I last wrote of the family because he had not swum into our ken.

We liked him instantly when he came down one week-end just before they got engaged. On that occasion, he presented me with Supradyne — a vitamin concoction — guaranteed to do a power of good when taken every morning (one tablet in water).

A few months later he approached me one week-end when they arrived from London. I was pouring out a drink as he asked me for Dinah's hand. I willingly conceded it to him on the condition that he promised to give me a monthly gift of Supradyne for ever. He agreed to this and has fulfilled the contract ever since, including when he was in the West Indies on his honeymoon — a couple of tubes turning up for father-in-law from a London chemist with a standing order.

Which reminds me that, when he had left the room to join Rachel and Dinah who were sharing the good news next door, Dinah came in and said reprovingly, 'Daddy, you never asked him how much money he had.' 'And why should I?' I enquired. 'It's you he's marrying, not me.' This seemed to me to be a logical conclusion to arrive at.

'Why aren't you sad?' she enquired of me, on the way to the church in a hired Daimler.

'Why should I be?' I asked her. 'That young man's delightful and you're going to be extremely happy.'

'Yes,' she said, 'but what about you losing your beloved little daughter?'

Cheeky little daughter, too!

I end this chapter with a favourite tale about my mother. This has already been published in my last book (or the one before!). She went to Edinburgh one day to buy a wedding present and, as was her custom, stuck a piece of writing paper down her corsage to prevent car-sickness. Having selected her purchase she asked the man behind the counter to send her the account. 'Yes, of course, my lady. Your address please?' Then he went straight on. 'All right my lady, I'll take it down from there,' he said, pointing towards the headed paper protruding from the top of her blouse.

CHAPTER 4

M y wife's relations — Brands first, and then Seeleys —
and the reason why she has a different name from me
will form the subject of this chapter.

Rachel Brand was how I knew her when I first met
her. Since then her name, once Mrs Douglas Home, has
changed again to Lady Dacre. This can on occasion provide some
embarrassment to both of us.

Staying the week-end in some quiet hotel, in which
our fellow guests regard us, I hope, as a delightful married
couple, things are apt to change when, as we are sitting quietly
at our table over dinner, the hotel intercom breaks in upon the
placid scene and requests Lady Dacre to go to the telephone.

I sit there in her absence, hot and bothered, knowing
that the eyes of all my fellow-diners are upon me, and
that all of them are now convinced that, far from being a happily
married couple, two of their fellow guests are, in fact, a thoroughly
immoral pair enjoying an illicit week-end.

When, some minutes later, she returns and takes her
seat again, eyes wink and heads nod around the tables,
registering a unanimous agreement that the call can only have
been from an outraged husband — called, presumably, Lord
Dacre!

I remember an evening of embarrassment when, on
boarding the *QE2* en route for the United States to see my
play *The Kingfisher*, starring Claudette Colbert and Rex Harrison,
our cabin door had only my name on it. This made me suspicious,
and sure enough, on opening the door, I saw an invitation lying on
the bed, addressed to me alone, and not my wife. We opened it to
find an invitation to the Captain's cocktail party that night. Once
we had settled in, I called the Captain's secretary and pointed out
that my wife had a different name from me. After some time she
called me back and told me to bring my wife along.

The Captain shook hands with us a little nervously —
no doubt assuming, as I thought in my imaginative mood,

that I was *bona fide* but that I had brought a girl along with me called Rachel Dacre, who was obviously not my wife. In spite of this, the voyage passed most pleasantly.

Here enters a new character — none other than Professor Trevor-Roper who, at one stage in his life, saw fit to further confuse an already awkward situation. He called up Rachel one fine morning when we were in Polzeath, staying with Celia Johnson. I was having breakfast with my hostess when the call came through. Rachel was not there because the evening before she had scratched her hand while peeling mussels, to which seafood she is totally allergic.

'It's Hugh Trevor-Roper, and he wants to speak to Rachel,' Celia informed me.

'Well, he can't,' I said.

'You take it then,' said Celia. I got up from the table and went over to the telephone.

'It's William, Hugh, not Rachel,' I said. 'She's in bed with mussel poisoning.'

'Oh, I'm so sorry,' said he. 'I was ringing just to tell her I've been made a life peer and I want to call myself Lord Dacre, as I had an ancestor who, like you, wed a Lady Dacre.'

'Hold on,' I said, 'I'll go and tell her.'

I got up, went along the passage and shouted through the bathroom door, 'Hugh Trevor-Roper wants to talk to you. He wants to call himself Lord Dacre.'

'I'll ring him back,' she answered weakly.

Back I went along the corridor, picked up the telephone and said, 'I'm sorry, Hugh, but she says she'll ring you back as soon as possible.'

'All right,' said he, 'but I won't be in long.' Then he rang off. Later in the morning, Rachel rang him back but, as he had predicted, he was not in.

Later still, he rang her back to say he hoped that she was feeling better, and that meanwhile he had been to see the Garter King at Arms who had expressed himself as being unperturbed by his request since there was a Lord Dacre in the House of Lords already (an ex-Labour MP who became a life peer). Thus did Lord Dacre of Glanton join Rachel in the

House of Lords — not wholly to her pleasure, since she does not like his name appearing in the papers, as it often does, without 'of Glanton' after it.

Another side-effect of his elevation is that a lot of letters come to me addressed to the Right Honourable Lord Dacre (sometimes with 'of Glanton' on the end, and sometimes not). These I return to him at great expense — I invariably open them on the assumption that those in the House of Lords who forward mail consider that, since I am Lady Dacre's husband (the hereditary Dacre, not the life peer), they must be for me.

Indeed I share that view myself, being convinced that, if the contents of the Sexual Discrimination Act were properly applied, I, being the consort of an hereditary peer, would in fact be called Lord Dacre.

I once did a good turn to Dacre (he of Glanton) when I wrote a letter to *The Times* after his Hitler's diaries trouble, saying that he might well be correct in his assumption that Hitler had written them (although the writer had used post-war ink and post-war paper) in retirement in the Argentine!

I like to think that, in return, he may one day rise in 'the other place' and move a motion calling for the husbands of hereditary peers to be allowed to take their consorts' names from henceforth!

Now for the Brand family, the forebears of my wife on her paternal side.

According to my good friend Jakie Astor's mother, Lady Astor, the Brands originally came from Europe. I suspect that she invented this but I recall her leaning over our son Jamie's pram when he was one year old and nodding her head sagely and then saying, 'Yes, typical German Brandt, I thought so.'

What a woman she was — but I mean to deal with her more fully in some later chapter. Meanwhile, for the record, I will only comment here that Bob Brand, the younger brother of 'Pop' Hampden — Rachel's grandfather — had married Lady Astor's sister, Phyllis, so conceivably she had a mischievous desire at one time or another to pull Bob's leg. Bob was a delightful man, as was his elder brother 'Pop' who wrote as follows to his mother from South Africa, where he was serving as a young Hussar in the Boer War: 'Worst day of the war so far. The port did not come up till after midnight.'

In his later years, after his wife's death, 'Pop' lived with my parents-in-law. One day Rachel's mother (*née* Seeley) went into the garden to check on how work on a new terrace was progressing. Stepping back onto the lawn to get a better view, she tripped over a plank and landed in the goldfish pond in the mink she was wearing to go up to London. 'Pop', who was in his bathroom upstairs, heard the splash while he was shaving, looked out of the window, raised the sash and shouted, 'Do it again, Leila, I just missed it.'

'Pop' had married into the Scott family, so my wife's father, Tommy Brand, was half-Scotch and half-English; when 'Pop' died, he succeeded to the Hampden title, which had been bestowed on Mr Speaker Brand in the last century.

So it seems that the Brand family harboured a title long before the days when Mr Speaker Brand became a peer but never got their hands on it till Gertrude, who presumably lacked brothers, came along and married Robert. And even when they had it, it stayed in abeyance until Tommy, Rachel's father, died without male issue.

After Tommy's death at too early an age, the title went to his brother David, who has since been succeeded by his son, Anthony, who lives at Glynde Place in East Sussex.

I rang up Anthony to find out why Dacre was included in the Hampden family, since he is very erudite about the family — indeed he wrote a book about it. Once he had finished telling me about a winner he had backed at Goodwood at twenty-five to one, he vouchsafed the information that, in the late eighteenth century, one Robert Brand had married Gertrude, Lady Dacre.

But to revert to 'Pop' and his generation: Bob, his younger brother who had married Phyllis Langhorne, was a member of the Milner Kindergarten in South Africa in his youth and then became (unlike 'Pop', except on occasion on the racecourse) a financial wizard in the City.

Admiral Sir Hubert Brand was yet another of 'Pop's' brothers. The story goes that when he was given command of the Home Fleet, and had stepped onto his flagship's quarter-deck for the first time and was standing proudly there, he was handed his first signal. It was from his brothers, and the message read as follows: 'If the British public knew you as we know you, they would not sleep easy in their beds tonight.'

Rachel's father, Tommy, was equally effective as his uncle Bob in the world of finance, and became Chairman of Lazard's Bank. I have written elsewhere of how well and helpfully he understood the hazards which are part and parcel of the theatre. When he died I lost a good friend who had taken the successes and the flops of my profession with impartial equanimity and sometimes on the chin.

His brother David did his best to fill the gap my father-in-law left. Indeed, one day, I well remember that he took me out to lunch and told me unequivocally that I should give up writing plays, since I was registering flops too frequently, and get myself another job. This could have been extremely sound advice (although I would have found it hard to follow) had I not a day or two later sold an option on *The Secretary Bird*.

Seeley was my mother-in-law Leila's maiden name. The family hails from Nottinghamshire and is noted both for coal-owning and for chasing foxes. One could argue with conviction that the word eccentric must have been invented to describe this family, since they are curiously unlike anybody else's, with only a few exceptions. They have charm, intelligence and beauty on the distaff side, while almost all the Seeley males that I have met, though perhaps lacking in beauty, share the first two qualities.

My mother-in-law's nephews, second cousins and the like include a gun-maker (Richard Beaumont), a clerk of the course at Ascot (Nicky Beaumont), a racing correspondent (Michael Seeley), another racing man of note (Brough Scott), as well as Michael Seeley's brother, Tim, who is an actor — all of which jobs, one assumes, are best performed by those who exercise their charm intelligently and their intelligence with charm.

As for Leila herself, all sons-in-law, or so convention has it, are allergic to their mothers-in-law and vice versa. In my own case I like to think that this is not true, even though I irritate her quite acutely sometimes. More often than not this is in retaliation for her irritating me — most notably when she sits too long over dinner, both in her own house and mine, because she does not wish to leave the men.

On such occasions I remove the plates sometimes, and risk the wrath which may fall on me for being interfering. But we manage to survive these things — which speaks well for her tolerance, when one considers that I tell her story after story about mothers-in-law when sitting beside her. For example, that told of Lord Justice Russell, who was stopped by a young barrister as he entered the Law Courts. 'Please remind me, my lord,' said the young man, 'before I go into court, what is the maximum penalty for bigamy?'

'Having two mothers-in-law,' replied the Lord Chief Justice, helpfully.

I wrote a play once called *And Her Mother Came Too*, which Leila came to see at the Thorndyke Theatre in Leatherhead. It even had a mouse-trap in it. But she took this on the chin, indomitable lady that she is. She will be ninety in the summer of the year in which I write this, sharing her birth-year with the Queen Mother, who is nearly three weeks younger.

This intrepid lady and my father-in-law Tommy had four daughters, two of whom died in their early years. The two who survived are my wife and her younger sister, Tessa, of whom we see far too little. She lives in South Africa and has four children, two sons and two daughters (and three grandchildren to date). Her husband, whom she met at Oxford, when she was at finishing school there, was a Rhodes Scholar at Worcester College. He is now Chairman of Anglo-American as well as of De Beers — which makes me feel, as I informed him recently, as though I were related to the Duke of Edinburgh and Mr Gorbachev combined.

The member of my mother-in-law's family whom I knew best was her half-sister, Sheila. She was married to Dick Talbot who, along with my mother's brothers, Johnny and Claud, was one of my favourite uncles.

He it was who hired himself a video which he found hard to master, even though I and my youngest daughter, Dinah, did our best to help him. One night, coming home to watch a cup tie that he had recorded, he switched on and found himself watching Sir John Betjeman reciting poetry. He took this on the chin, but a fortnight later he switched on to watch some race at Newmarket that he had videoed and found himself faced with Sir John again, reciting the same poetry. Although a patient man, this was too much for him. Next morning, he got into his car, drove to Petersfield at speed and handed the delinquent tape in, pointing out that all that it recorded was Sir John. The girl behind the counter gave him a new tape — eternal credit to her.

Uncle Dick was passionate in his youth, according to Aunt Sheila. I discovered this when she lunched with us one day after his death.

The conversation had ranged around 'the Ruthven Twins', two beauties of the Twenties, when Aunt Sheila intervened. 'Dick fell in love with one of them,' she said in her inimitable drawl.

'What happened?' I enquired.

'Oh, nothing really,' Sheila said. And then she paused and added, 'Well, he did put stones in his pockets actually and then walked onto Westminster Bridge.'

'Yes,' I said, excitedly, 'then what?'

'He changed his mind,' she answered, buttering her roll, 'thank goodness.'

So much for the Seeleys. I suppose my four children all have certain eccentricities inherited through their Seeley blood, though many argue that Seeley eccentricities are nothing to Lambton eccentricities. Yet although Jack Durham, the twin elder brother of my mother's father, did marry a girl in London who went mad in the train on the way to Lambton Castle for the honeymoon, this unhappy fact did not augment the Lambton eccentricity in any way because the marriage was not consummated. When they arrived in Newcastle, the bride was taken off to an asylum where she spent the remainder of her life. Thus any rumour that the Lambton blood was tainted at that time (I emphasize the phrase 'at that time') is unfounded. Any later eccentricities which came into the family came after my mother's birth.

CHAPTER 5

The families around us in the Border Country whom we knew best were those of aunts or uncles, such as the Dundases. Sir Henry Dundas was one of my godfathers. He had lots of sons, all dead now, and one daughter, Jean, who married Peter Reid, an admiral and the son of Sir James Reid, one of Queen Victoria's most trusted doctors.

Peter and Jean had a daughter who is married to David Montgomery (not the Field Marshal's son), whose house is at the west end of Loch Leven. They in turn have a young daughter, Mrs Humphrey Butler, who made daughter Dinah's wedding dress last year. I mention this to show how close the family connections still remain.

The other Border relatives were on my mother's side. They included the Egertons, the children of my mother's sister Violet (the subject of the telegram that landed Uncle Claud in trouble, mentioned earlier) and Joan, another sister of my mother's and the wife of Hugh Joicey, who lived just across the Tweed at Etal, near to Uncle Johnny — not to mention Uncle Claud, Aunt Olive and their daughter Barbara.

Olive was a warm and cheerful lady who took no offence when one of my father's fishermen, Jimmy Scott, who was then in his eighties, spoke to her in rather forceful terms after she had hooked an autumn salmon of substantial size one morning on the Lower Water.

'Hold the point of your rod up, you silly old bitch,' was the phrase he used according to Aunt Olive, who had no reason to lie, nor anything but gratitude for advice which helped her to secure her trophy.

Uncle Johnny (Durham), mother's eldest brother, lived at Fenton with his second wife, Hermione — his first wife having died young after giving birth to Roddy (who also died young) and to Tony — who is now known as Lord Lambton, even though he gave up the Durham title when he inherited it and, on his own initiative, passed it to his son. I must confess I fail to understand how this has come about, but come about it has, and seems to be in keeping with the fact that he is an eccentric fellow.

No one else that I can think of except Tony would have visited a house of ill fame in his government car, flying its official flag. Weaker mortals like myself would have taken a taxi. That is why I have a secret admiration for him.

But to get back to my close relatives: when my sister Rachel married Billy Scott, the MP for Roxburgh and Selkirk, the family enlarged its numbers still further, bringing in the whole Scott family from Walter Buccleuch, Billy's brother, his wife Molly and their children, Johnny, Elizabeth and Caroline — as well as some character-full cousins of theirs, such as Andrew Scott who married Dozia, sister of Dawick Haig.

Andrew was a most amusing man. Two tales about him that I cherish concern his wartime career. The background to the first was Norway, where he found himself in 1940, just before the British forces were evacuated from that country. He was about to board a cruiser when his servant (so-called in the Guards, rather than a batman) told him that a hot bath had been run in a house nearby which had just been evacuated at speed by the Swedish Minister.

Andrew, who was a colonel in the Irish Guards, took advantage of his servant's find; he went into the house, undressed and sank into the bath, a luxury that he had not indulged in for some days (or was it weeks?).

After he had got out he dried himself and went back into the bedroom — where he caught sight of a petticoat with butterflies embroidered on it lying on the double bed, abandoned by the Swedish Minister's wife in the rush of her departure. He was about to put on his vest and pants when he noticed that they were in a very bad state, so he donned the petticoat instead, and put on his battledress again.

As he left the house, his servant told him that it was time to board the cruiser, which was lying at the quay a hundred yards or so away. Once on board, Andrew was shown to a cabin where, since it was on the warm side, he took off his battledress again and lay down on the bunk, smoking a large cigar.

Some minutes later, came a knock at the door. Andrew called 'come in'. It opened, and the captain of the cruiser came in saying 'Colonel Scott, I wondered if you'd care to dine —' the voice then stopped abruptly as the captain saw the petticoated figure through the smoke of the cigar, turned on his heel and shut the door, leaving the invitation to dine unconfirmed.

That was the last time Andrew met the captain because, ever after, when he saw him either in the street in London or at some reunion, he took evasive action.

Andrew's father, Lord Herbert Scott, was the Chairman of Rolls-Royce. According to report, he had a large family, apart from his own, in some convenient London suburb. This was confirmed to me by my late father-in-law, who once saw his uncle in a theatre in the row just in front of him, accompanied by a strange lady and a lot of children.

My father never spoke about this relationship because such matters were not in his line of conversation, but he got on well with both George and Henry Scott, Lord Herbert's brothers, although John Buccleuch, their eldest brother, awed him somewhat since — and I can vouch for this myself — he always wore a bowler hat at meals.

Lord George was a good fellow, although he once shocked my father when I was a small boy. As he left the shooting-brake, he called back to my forebear, 'Charlie, chuck me out the Holy Ghost' — and then added, having noted that my father looked surprised, 'My Comforter.'

Lord Henry was a bachelor who lived in a house called Gledswood on the Tweed below 'Scott's View' — a spot on the road running just above the river where the horses harnessed to Sir Walter Scott's hearse stopped on their way to the cemetery, just as they always had when pulling their employer's carriage in his lifetime.

It seems likely that he had composed his well-known lines about the Eildon Hill on that spot:

> 'Three peaks against the saffron sky
> Beneath the purple plain
> That well-remembered melody
> Of Tweed — once more again.'

The last line may not perhaps be Sir Walter's best, but the picture it conveys is wholly accurate.

When the bowler-hatted John Buccleuch passed on, his eldest son, Walter Dalkeith, succeeded him.

He was one of the nicest men I ever met, and even though it may be argued — and perhaps with some truth — that I say that about everyone, he totally deserved such a description since his kindness, his charm and his sense of humour were, all three of them, outstanding.

He had been a Tory MP for a large part of his life — indeed, I rather think my brother-in-law, Billy Scott, took over from him when he went to the Lords after John Buccleuch's death. He much endeared himself to me — although I knew nothing of it at the time — by trying, during the War, to mitigate the ill-effects of Unconditional Surrender by pursuing peace-feelers from Germany through Switzerland and elsewhere. These never came to anything because of the Prime Minister's total addiction to that policy.

Among the Germans who tried to contact Walter, sometimes successfully, were many of those who attempted to get rid of Hitler in the 1944 July Plot. If contacts with such people had been made by members of the Government instead of by individuals, they might well have gained the necessary support to get the entire German army on their side, instead of only certain generals who did their best to help — like Rommel, for example, who paid with his life for doing so.

In later life, Walter enjoyed himself, largely in Scotland, in the company of Molly, his attractive wife.

The story goes that, in his youth, he was chosen to be the consort of the Princess Royal, and was summoned down to Windsor by her parents with a view to urging him to take her on.

Some say that he went down by train, took a taxi to the Castle, lost his nerve when he observed Queen Mary waiting for him on the doorstep, told the taxi-driver to return to Windsor Station, and hurried back to London. There, or so I've heard it said, he went round to Molly's home, where he proposed to her through the bathroom door, beyond which he could hear the sound of the running taps. To his relief, he was instantly accepted.

Johnny, his son, married Jane MacNeill who bore him four delightful children, all of whom make sure that he enjoys the life he has to spend in a bath-chair as a result of his horse falling at a stone wall when he was out hunting with his own hounds in the Border land some years ago.

His sister Caroline is married to Sir Ian Gilmour, who was one of the first casualties of Mrs Thatcher's leadership — an independent-minded Tory MP who is both good-looking and intelligent (which does not go for all of them!).

The eldest of the three, Elizabeth Northumberland, was married to a school-fellow of mine, Hughie Northumberland.

It is said that some facetious boy informed Hughie on his first day at Eton that when his housemaster came round to say goodnight to him it was an old-established custom to enquire of him what buggery was — a word Hughie had not heard at that stage in his life. In consequence, he had no hesitation about doing as he had been told.

Mr Adie, his housemaster, came into his room that night and enquired, 'Is everything all right?'

'Yes, quite all right, sir,' Hughie answered.

'Good,' said Mr Adie, turning for the door — at which Hughie added, 'Sir, what's buggery?'

His housemaster turned round, looked at him to see if he was joking in a thoroughly precocious manner, decided that he wasn't, and said 'Oscar Wilde got two or three years for it, didn't he?' He then added 'Goodnight, Percy,' shut the door, and went into the night.

Hughie, who died a few years back, had a quiet sense of humour and laughed so much when he was engaged in telling one a story that it was not always easy to pick up the gist of it. One such concerned the time when Elizabeth told him that Michael Redgrave would be coming from Newcastle for tea at Alnwick Castle, as he wanted to look at some volumes of Shakespeare in the library.

She went on to say that she could not be there herself to entertain him as she had to be at a meeting, so would Hughie entertain him in her stead when he got back from hunting.

Sure enough, at half past four precisely, Hughie came in to find Michael Redgrave waiting for him. They had tea together, during which he gave his guest a lecture on the subject of the Bard, informing him that he had lived at Stratford-upon-Avon and that he had written lots of plays, giving the names of some of them and outlining their plots.

When he thought that his visitor was primed sufficiently, he took him to the library, where he showed him the rare volumes he had come to see. While Michael Redgrave was inspecting them, Hughie continued with his Shakespeare lecture, telling him how his family had acquired the volumes he was studying.

The session over, Redgrave thanked him for his tea and for allowing him to visit the library. Hughie took him to the door and saw him off, then went to have his after-hunting rest. Some time later Elizabeth woke him up and asked him how the visit had gone.

'Very well,' said Hughie. 'He seemed very interested in what I told him about Shakespeare.'

'What *you* told *him*!' cried Elizabeth.

'Yes,' Hughie said. 'I thought he ought to know what he was looking at.' Then, as she gasped for breath, he went on, 'Anyway, who was the fellow?'

'I told you this morning, Hughie,' said Elizabeth. 'He's Michael Redgrave.'

'Oh, I didn't hear you,' Hughie said. 'What does he do?'

Then when she told him that he was in Newcastle that week performing Shakespeare, Hughie merely said, 'Well, why didn't he say so?', closed his eyes and relived his day's hunting in his mind before sleep overtook him once again.

Writing of Alnwick puts me in mind of Jamie McEwen. On one occasion Jamie and I travelled down to Alnwick by train from Berwick-on-Tweed for a day's shooting and the Percy hunt ball.

As the taxi drove towards the entrance to the Castle, Jamie put his collar up.

'Why are you doing that?' I asked him.

'A precaution against boiling oil,' he told me.

Another local neighbour was Sir Eric de la Rue, a kindly, absent-minded fellow who lived at Lennel, down the Tweed beyond Coldstream.

The way he got engaged to Betty Sitwell's sister always intrigued me. During the War, in his army days, he was on sentry duty outside some important requisitioned building in Grosvenor Square one morning when a young girl of his acquaintance, for whom he had a profound affection, walked by on the pavement.

'Pussy,' he called — Pussy being her pet-name, Waring her surname. She stopped and looked up at Eric, not knowing that he was stationed in town.

'Hullo Eric,' she said.

'Come and have lunch with me,' said Eric.

'But aren't you on sentry duty?' Pussy asked.

'Yes, but never mind that,' Eric replied — at which he leaned his rifle, with fixed bayonet, up against the wall behind him, hurried down the steps, and took her off to lunch at Claridge's.

On his return, much fortified by food and wine, as well as being engaged, he picked up his rifle and went off to meet his sergeant-major, who was waiting for him.

One day he came to lunch at Springhill with my mother before going pigeon-shooting. During the meal, he said to her, 'By the way, I've got a present for you, Lady Home.' At that, he put his hand into his pocket and pulled out a small white mouse, which he held out towards her.

'Put that thing away at once,' she told him sharply. This he did, and then continued with the meal.

When his wife Pussy died he wed another charming lady who, in Eric's old age, had a baby by another man. Asked by some newspaper reporter on the telephone how he reacted to this escapade, he said, 'I don't like babies — they're always breaking up the furniture,' and left it at that.

It was to Cranshaws, Stennard Landale's rented house in the Lammermuirs, that Rachel and I came after our long honeymoon in Italy, writing a film script. On our first night home, after supper, we moved into the sitting-room to find my labrador asleep on the grand-piano, which had been thrown in with the house. We soon discovered that he had adopted this position because of the draught across the floor. Then winter came, and with it Jamie, our first child.

Next year we left Cranshaws, Stennard Landale letting me off the rent for the final quarter of my lease, and moved to Jakie Astor's dower house at Hartley Park near Gamlingay (in which he now lives himself). After that we lived for thirty years at Drayton House, East Meon — four or five miles from our new home, in which I sit writing this.

Visits to Scotland still continued, most of them to my old friend George Lansdowne. His home at Meikleour boasts a famous beech hedge, which used to be cut by the fire brigade every year — nowadays other means have to be employed, since it has grown too high for fire-ladders.

Both the shooting and the fishing were outstanding at Meikleour, though the latter is rather different from that practised on the Tweed. The stream is so strong that the boat needs an engine rather than an oarsman, though Tay fishermen are just as necessary and as highly skilled as their colleagues on the Tweed.

The technique involves driving the boat into the correct position and then dropping the anchor, which is attached to a rope which slowly lets the boat down as the fisherman casts to right or left, according to his orders, with a fly or, if the river is on the big side and dirty, a spoon or a golden sprat.

This technique is not often unrewarded. Indeed, I have been told by the proprietor that he sometimes requires his tenants to put back every salmon they catch once they have landed twenty!

Although such catches have been known on the Tweed, they are hardly commonplace.

Another thing that happens on the Tay, but not on the Tweed, is 'harling', which consists of throwing out a long line and leaving it there while the fisherman, helped by both oars and engine, zig-zags his boat up-stream with the line trailing out behind it.

In the days when George still owned the high ground, before he passed it on to Charlie, his heir, as he did with Bowood in the south, the shooting at Meikleour was varied, consisting of duck, geese, snipe, grouse and pheasants.

Before the War, and for a long time thereafter, the keeper at Meikleour was a Mr Finlay. Hours spent with him in a stubble-field waiting for geese were well-rewarded, since his conversation was enthralling and his knowledge of the birds and beasts that surrounded us was unrivalled.

Mention of Mr Finlay reminds me once again of my father's keeper, Mr Telfer. He was another character — totally upstanding, honest and outspoken. Like Mr Finlay he made every shoot enjoyable and every grouse-drive an adventure.

My most favourite story about him concerns the time when he was on his way home from a session in the Douglas Arms in Douglas village on a Saturday night, having had a few too many. Some miners on their way to work on the early morning shift came across him lying, passed out, on the side of the track. Since most of them had been had up by him for poaching rabbits in the past, they thought it would be in order to extract a mild revenge, given such a golden opportunity. They picked him up, carried him a mile or so to a Douglas water pit, took him down the shaft and waited for him to come round. The following Monday Mr Telfer told my father about this episode in the most picturesque terms — 'When I came to, my lord, I looked up at those black faces peering down at me and thought that I was in the next world!'

But back to Perthshire, after that little diversion. When I was just out of my teens, I shot fifty-six duck early one morning flight on what was called the little loch, adjacent to Blairgowrie golf course. At the same time, the butts on the big loch were filled by George's stepfather, John Astor, and his friend, Lord Winchelsea. The latter later told his host over breakfast that he had to 'reach out a bit' for the ducks — another way of saying that he had shot at them too high, so diverting them towards the little loch, where I was waiting. My bag of fifty-six was — and still is — a record for a morning's flight, which may explain why I have not forgotten those two early morning hours from more than fifty years ago.

Goose-shooting was another entertainment practised at a bend in the Tay just above Meikleour. Here on cold and frosty evenings, one would lie and listen for the greylags calling, on their way back from the stubbles where they had spent the day. First heard a mile or so away, their cackling came ever closer. Finally one heard the swishing of their wings, as they dived in to roost in some back-water.

Never mind how few geese were bagged on such evenings, it was always thrilling to hear their wild cries, high in the starlit sky as they flew up the river and came in on course.

Once, I remember Michael Astor, my friend Jakie's brother and my best man at my wedding, failed to join our party in the darkness as we wended our way homewards down the river bank. We went back to look for him, fearing that he might have fallen in, only to hear the sound of digging, coming from a muddy piece of ground below the steep bank.

We pressed on, looked over the bank and, by the light of the moon, saw Michael burying a swan which he had fired at in mistake for a goose. As a penalty, George made him carry the vast bird all the way home. I think it likely that that was the last swan Michael ever shot at.

Another of my favourite stories concerns one of George's keepers, who used to come down from Tullybeagles to help Mr Finlay on big shooting days. Perhaps because he came from the high tops, Mr Redfern was less easygoing than Mr Finlay, demanding of his beaters more than one would ask of those on the plains.

One day, as I was walking on the left of the line down a stubble-field, I saw the beater on my flank, who was engaged in driving out a marshy piece of ground with his colleagues, wade into a pool of water under some willows almost up to his neck. Thinking this well beyond the call of duty, I was just about to suggest to him that he should not be so dangerously conscientious when the voice of Mr Redfern rang out from a hillock at the other end of the line. 'Wullie,' it cried, 'can ye no' do better than that!'

Alas, there are no more invitations from Meikleour for the pheasant shooting, now that George has decided to hang up his cartridge bag. His friends, like Michael Lyle and John Nelson and myself, protested violently, but to no avail. Unmoved by our impassioned pleas, he gave his twelve-bores to his grandson and then let his shooting, even though the rent that he acquires from doing so is — as I never cease telling him — equivalent to coals to Newcastle. Instead he wanders round his land all day and spends a lot of time in the new woodland garden that he has created downstream from his house.

George is descended from one Comte de Flauhert, an illegitimate son of Monsieur Talleyrand. He married a Scots lassie called Miss Mercer Elphinstone, who owned the land around Meikleour at that time. George is proud of his French ancestry and speaks the language with great fluency — so well that he was chosen as liaison officer to General Le Clerc, when he marched a Free French force up from Dakar in the middle of the War.

We still see George a lot, however. He asks us up for the

fishing, and we also see him when we stay with David Perth, who lives across the river from him and most kindly asks me to shoot every other year.

One of the disenfranchised guns I mentioned earlier is Michael Lyle, who lives at Reimore near Dunkeld. The one- or two-mile drive leading up to his house in the hills provides entertainment every inch of the way — roe deer feeding on the roadside, red deer further up the hill, and ospreys, peregrines and even eagles frequently appearing in the sky above.

Michael is a strong Liberal, as is his wife Elizabeth. She is the daughter of Sir Archibald Sinclair, who was leader of the Liberal Party — as well as being Air Minister in Sir Winston's wartime Government (the same one that it was my wartime ambition to bring down!).

When Michael was a wee laddie he was taken out one day by the head stalker, on his father's orders, so that he could learn the rudiments of stalking from him. They were eating their lunch beside a wall that ran down to a loch, when the old man turned to Michael and said, 'Master Michael, do ye see yon mound away behind the birches on the far side of the loch?'

'Yes,' Michael said.

'Well,' went on the head stalker, 'when I was a lad like you, I saw the Queen through my glass walk out from yon trees and squat behind yon mound and lift her skirts. Aye, that was something.'

Evidently the Queen and Prince Albert had been travelling back to Balmoral from Blair Atholl where they had been staying while the former was being refurbished. Indeed, they stayed there so long, or so the story runs, that, as a reward, they gave the Duke of Atholl of the day the right to form a private army, which his successor still commands.

Mention of that earlier Duke reminds me of the story of when, in his later years, he was walking home with his head stalker, Donald, from a day on the hill.

As they approached the low ground, the Duke said to Donald, 'Donald, that was my last day on the hill.' 'That's a lot of nonsense, your Grace,' Donald said. 'You're no' all that old. There's a lot of stalking in you yet.'

'No, Donald, it's not that,' the Duke explained. 'My wife went to a doctor down in London recently and he said she must spend the autumn and the winter in the South of France from now on. And, of course, I will be going with her.'

Silence reigned for some time, as they walked on, until the Duke heard the voice of Donald, who walking right behind him, saying clearly and distinctly, 'The bitch!'

George's other friend, John Nelson, whom I mentioned earlier, was joint school bookie with George when they were at Eton. They avoided capture by suggesting to Giles Alington, the son of Dr Cyril, the Headmaster, that he should wager a sixpence on the outcome of the Eton and Harrow match that summer. Giles agreed to do this. George and John recorded the bet in their betting book.

In consequence, whenever any enterprising and suspicious master found the telltale book while George and John were absent from their rooms, the routine was that he would open up the book in great excitement, find on the first page (since Alington begins with an A) the record of young Giles's bet, then close it hurriedly and keep his lips securely sealed thereafter.

Years later, when he had become a general, John found himself in charge of Rudolph Hess in Spandau Prison when he was in command in West Berlin.

Once, during a game of bridge, John told me that the first time he went to see Rudolph Hess, he made him laugh.

'How did you manage that?' I asked him, as I tried to play the hand.

'Well,' said John, 'when I asked if he had any complaints, he said "Yes". So I said, "Well, what are they?" And he told me that he wanted to spend more time in the garden.'

'Well, why don't you?' John enquired.

'Because they think I'm mad,' said Hess.

'And are you?' John asked.

'No,' said Hess.

'In that case,' John said, 'I'll let you spend more time there — at least until I find you watering the garden when it's raining.'

At that, Hess began to laugh and went on doing so whenever he met John thereafter.

As I mentioned in an earlier book, my mother saw Herr Hess's Messerschmidt fly past her bedroom window on its way to Moffat, where its pilot parachuted out. My mother, who was tidying her hair before her evening meal, went down and told my father that she had seen a strange-looking aeroplane flying westwards over the lake.

Next morning they both heard the news that Rudolph Hess had flown to see the Duke of Hamilton.

I heard the news in Kingsbridge, Devon, where my regiment was stationed, and my heart leapt in anticipation of what I had longed for every waking hour since the War started, namely a negotiated peace. But it was not to be at that time, nor at any other, because Winston Churchill's policy of Unconditional Surrender made it necessary for the War to continue to the end.

When that end came, I found myself in Wakefield Prison listening to the Prime Minister reporting that the German War was over, on the radio. In the next chapter, I propose to follow the strange route that took me there.

CHAPTER 6

A nd now to graver matters, and a more serious chapter. In three years' time it will be fifty years since I arrived in Wormwood Scrubs to start my sentence for refusing to obey an order in the field in 1944. Yet even now the story is not over.

In order to provide the reader with some background information, I propose to trace the influences which, in early youth and later, sowed the seeds which ultimately yielded up so strange a crop.

The first of these concerns my father's absence from home during the First World War. I found it hard to visualize a situation in which any man as charming as he was could want to go and kill a lot of other men with little children of their own — men like the German prisoners-of-war who laid drains down the roadside outside Springhill. Later, at Eton, I found bayonet practice an unedifying sport, made more so by the intervention of the sergeant-major, whose imagination sometimes led him to indulge himself beyond the call of duty in descriptive comments of a most unpleasant nature. Sometimes these amused me but, at other times, when I was in a contemplative mood, they so revolted me that one day I decided that I would be happier if I left the Corps — a step which my superiors most willingly connived at. Later still, at Oxford, I read history, and found myself not always totally convinced by the arguments put forward by politicians of the past to excuse their participation in whatever wars occurred during their period of office. When it came to being on the side of Fox or Pitt, I invariably chose the former or, in the next century, Lord Lansdowne rather than the government of Mr Lloyd George.

After I had left Oxford, during my time at RADA, in repertory and in the West End theatre, I used to write to the *Scotsman* on the subject of what I assumed — correctly, as it turned out — would be World War Two.

I chose the *Scotsman* for the simple reason that since my family lived in its circulation area, I hoped it might be readier to print my effusions than the London papers. It was. Written in the last few years before the War, my letters dealt with the prime necessity of making peace with Hitler or, if not with him, with those in Germany, in civil life or in the forces, who disliked him just as much as I did — quite a few of whom attempted to dislodge him in the July Plot of 1944.

Given my views, it is not surprising that, when called up as a conscript soldier in July 1940, I wrote to the Labour Exchange informing them that, although I had decided not to put myself forward as a Conscientious Objector because I could not guarantee that I would never kill anybody in self-defence, I could not promise that circumstances might not arise during the prosecution of the War in which, because of my views, I might not prove to be wholly reliable. This letter was not answered.

After my call-up I joined a training battalion of the 7th Buffs — the Royal West Kent Regiment — at Maidenhead. Some weeks later, we were removed to Kingsbridge, Devon. It was there that my colonel, Roscoe Reid, told me one morning that he was planning to send me off on an officer-training course. I told him that, though this would probably prove a disaster due to my deep-seated convictions about the folly of a prolonged war, I had to accede to his request since I had decided from the start to do my best in the army for as long as possible — in other words, until some situation arose which I felt bound to question.

Thus I found myself at Sandhurst, a month or so later, playing the part of an officer cadet. Once again, I felt it necessary to enlighten my instructors as to my political views in order to avoid misunderstandings. Being Guards officers, they were highly tolerant, only displaying unrest when it looked as though I might end up being posted to one or other of their regiments!

All attempts by various friends and well-wishers to get me into such exalted company having failed, I wrote to Colonel Reid down in Devonshire suggesting that he took me back beneath his wing, albeit in a different role.

Though far from happy at the prospect, he was a man of sterling character and he wrote back to say that he was prepared to accept me as a subaltern if no one else would. He also suggested that I gave up talking 'bloody politics' when I returned, and concentrated instead on being a soldier. Back I went to meet his baleful eye, the quips of his colleagues, and the cheerful ruderies of all my erstwhile comrades in the ranks, and I soldiered on in charge of signalling and entertainment for some time.

Before long, though, I had become incensed by the policy of Unconditional Surrender, as put forward by Churchill and Roosevelt. This seemed to me to run counter to the spirit of the 1941 Atlantic Charter, which had promised a fair deal for all nations — including enemy nations — in the post-war years. Why, I asked myself and anybody else who would listen, was it necessary to change from a policy which had held out hope for all to a policy guaranteed, whatever else it might achieve, to prolong the War?

Up rose my hackles and my political antennae — rising even higher in May 1941 with the news of Rudolph Hess's flight to Scotland in search of a compromise.

One day in 1942 I read in the newspapers of a by-election that was due to take place in Cathcart, Glasgow (which, incidentally, was the first seat Alec ever fought). I went to Colonel Reid and asked for his permission to declare myself a candidate. After launching into a tirade about 'bloody politicians', he accepted his adjutant's advice that, according to King's Regulations, he was bound to grant me my wish.

After some delay in clearing permission from the War Office, I found myself in Glasgow at last with only a few days left before polling day. After fighting on a policy of peace aims and less obstinacy on the part of Messrs Roosevelt and Churchill, I came second in a field of five.

A few months later, in June 1942, Windsor and Maidenhead lost their MP through death. Once again I put the question to Colonel Reid, and once again, encouraged by Arthur Majendie, his adjutant, he sent me on my way with imprecations and a twinkle in his eye.

Arrived in Windsor, as I have recounted earlier, I stood as an Independent against my old school friend, Charlie Mott Radclyffe. Supported by the Coalition Government, he beat me by 2,600 votes: but with over 6,000 votes cast on my behalf, I became even more convinced that many of the inhabitants of Windsor and

Maidenhead shared my longing for a less rigid approach to the problems of securing peace.

Some months later, another by-election loomed in St Albans, but permission from the Army Council failed to come through in time, much to my regret. In the event, the seat was won by an Independent, Raymond Blackburn, which increased my sense of frustration.

Then, two years later, just before the Second Front, I stood in Clay Cross, Derbyshire, which was a Labour stronghold. Inevitably, I lost my deposit, due to the fact that the Labour Party always closes rank with the opposition in an international crisis, regardless of the views it holds in peacetime, however sincere these may be.

I returned to my regiment having been quoted in the press as saying that I no longer regarded the War as just; and a few weeks later, I sailed in my tank-landing craft out of Gosport en route for the Second Front. Once in Normandy, my sense of disillusionment grew even stronger as I sat in the Reserve Squadron Tank harbour watching the bombing of Caen — a sight which convinced me that Unconditional Surrender was an even worse mistake than I had previously thought it to be. Offering no prospect of negotiation, what I saw at Caen compared unfavourably with the scenes that were taking place outside Cherbourg at about the same time: according to my later information, which I like to think was correct, the Americans besieging the town broadcast to the German occupying force that coffee was waiting for them if they came out peacefully. They did!

From this point on, my political opinions and my scruples about the War drew ever closer: so much so that I wrote to Colonel Waddell, my new colonel — Roscoe Reid had retired — asking him to allow me to resign my commission. I don't think he ever got around to forwarding this request to higher authority — but even if he did, nothing came of it. Nor did an alternative request on my part asking him to arrange my transfer to some political propaganda unit, which role might have suited my talents better than that of a fighting soldier, ever get off the ground.

I reached the point of no return outside Le Havre, early in September 1944, when I felt duty bound to disobey my colonel's order to proceed to C Squadron and act as a liaison officer between the infantry and our tanks when the battle to relieve the town began.

I told Colonel Waddell that I would not do so as our regimental intelligence officer had informed me that the commander of the German garrison had asked for permission to evacuate a large number of civilians from the town before the battle started, and that this request had been refused. Colonel Waddell told me to think again but I remained adamant. (I learned recently that the commander in Le Havre was not a regular Wehrmacht officer but a merchant banker who had joined the army at the outbreak of war. Maybe this accounted for his unusual approach.)

Be that as it may, his advances were rebuffed after our over-all commander — a Canadian, I believe — had refused to entertain the idea, thinking it a ruse by which the Germans hoped to delay an attempt to take the town while at the same time delaying repairs to the port, which the Allies desperately needed. This excuse did not seem to me to hold water, since the entire evacuation could have been completed in a day or less, and the Allied troops around Le Havre had already sat for three days doing nothing. It would have saved the lives of three thousand civilians, who died as a result of the British bombing raid on the town on the night of 5 September.

That, in a nut-shell, is the explanation for my refusal to obey orders. Many people have deplored it, saying to my face that any officer who takes the law into his own hands rather than obey his commanding officer deserves to be court-martialled. Some have openly accused me of cowardice, though others have congratulated me on doing something they would have liked to do themselves while doubting whether they would have been obstinate enough to go through with it. Most soldiers and ex-soldiers tend to see my point of view and do not censure it, at any rate to my face.

I learned this many years later, when a BBC team tried to tell the story of my war — a project with which I was ready to co-operate at first, but which was eventually abandoned. The organizers of the programme talked to many of my surviving fellow-officers and to non-commissioned officers and men in my regiment, most of whom thought I had a point.

Although I was flattered when I was told that I would be played by Daniel Day Lewis, this was not enough to persuade me to co-operate. I disliked the idea of my playing the leading role, albeit in disguise; I felt that the film should have been about Le Havre and the problems posed by the German commandant's request rather than about one very junior officer.

The promoters, who were very understanding, argued that the film would come out that way: but I didn't believe it, nor was I prepared to risk the accusation that I had allowed myself to play the hero in a film in which I should have played a minor role. For me to take such an attitude may seem to some people improbable, not to say entirely out of character, since there are those who look upon my penchant for publicity as an insatiable lust. But I like to think that I only court publicity when it seems to further some cause. Early this year, incidentally, a half-hour film about Le Havre was made by BBC Glasgow which earned my full approval.

As regards my refusal to obey that order at Le Havre, I had no shadow of doubt that, whatever publicity might result — and indeed did result, through my own efforts to secure it — could do nothing but good; which is why I wrote a letter to the press pointing out exactly what I did.

The paper I chose, the *Maidenhead Advertiser*, saw fit to give it banner headlines similar to the coverage they had given the by-election in 1944. It was also quoted widely in the national press.

As a result of this, my colonel felt obliged to arrange for my court-martial. Many people thought that I was foolish to have courted trouble quite deliberately. I was unperturbed however, since my purpose was to bring the whole affair into the open, in the hope that some good might result from doing so.

Encouraged by the fact that I had stirred up something, I sat down and wrote another letter to the *Advertiser*, which I like to think had some effect on future events. During all this period I was attached to HQ Squadron as a non-combatant officer.

Hardly had extracts from that letter been republished in the national press before news came that Allied troops attacking Calais had been asked by the German commanding officer in the town to allow him to evacuate all civilians. I also learned, to my delight, that his request had been granted by the Allied High Command. Out came the citizens of Calais, and soon afterwards — since they had been evacuated in a lot of German army lorries and the lorry-drivers had decided to stay where they were — the garrison surrendered *en masse*. Later on the same thing happened in Dunkirk.

When this news reached me, where I was billeted awaiting my court-martial, I cheered up immensely: I wondered whether someone in the High Command had not been made a little nervous by the fact that what had happened at Le Havre (or, rather, had not happened) had been made public, and whether this had possibly encouraged the German commanders in Calais and Dunkirk to make similar requests.

My court-martial took place on 4 October 1944 in Ghent, which at the time was close to our army headquarters. It began with an incident which amuses me now, though I don't think I found it very funny at the time. The judge advocate, Major Neild — of whom more later — read out my number, name and regiment, the first of which was incorrect.

He credited me with army number 175797. When I pointed out that, in fact, it was 176797 he turned to the president of the court and asked whether, under rule of procedure such-and-such, that mistake could be amended, to which the president replied 'Yes'. Had he replied 'No', of course, the whole proceedings would have been suspended on the grounds that the court was trying the wrong man!

The presiding officer (whose name always eludes my pen) then began his speech. He gave details of the meeting I had had with my commanding officer in which I had refused to take part in the battle of Le Havre. He then went on to say that he must be satisfied of three things: that the command was lawful; that it was given by a superior officer; and that it had been disobeyed.

Colonel Waddell, my commanding officer, was called and he confirmed the prosecution officer's description of the episode. He also said that he had had a letter from me asking if I could resign my commission, and that this was hanging fire at the time.

At this point, I asked him whether I had not discussed with him, in frequent letters and interviews, my aversion to having to fight in a war in which we faced our enemies with a demand for Unconditional Surrender. He agreed with this, but went on to say that he had thought my views about the War would not be the same on this side as they had been on the other side. By this, no doubt, he meant that he had assumed that arrival in the war zone would have rid me of my political and conscientious hang-ups and turned me into a dedicated soldier like himself, determined to destroy the enemy and not to parley with him. This approach, alas — however well it suited him — was not for me.

I was then called upon to take my place in the witness box. I began by attempting to explain what I was basing my defence on — namely that there were extenuating circumstances which should be allowed for.

I said that, from a purely selfish point of view, I was not particularly concerned about the charge against my honour, because I was satisfied that whatever impression might be given to the public by the decision of the court, I had done what I conceived to be right.

However, I went on to say that that decision, were it to condemn me, must affect the honour of my family. I then outlined the previous events in my life which had set me on the road to making such a stand, starting with an article I had written at school entitled 'Blessed are the Peace-Makers' and signed 'A Child of God'.

I went on to quote from a letter I had written to the *Scotsman* in May 1937 which ended as follows: 'The great democracies continue to confuse strategic moves with moral arguments. Could we not learn, before it is too late, that morality and strategy make uneasy bed-fellows and breed nothing but confusion and thus spare ourselves the ultimate hypocrisy?'

I told the court that I had met a German colonel in Germany in August 1939 and that he had said to me, 'There will be a war. I hate Hitler but I shall fight again. I can do nothing else, because I am a soldier.' I differed from my German friend in that I was not a soldier, but merely a civilian in battledress, who had warned the Labour Exchange, when my call-up papers arrived in 1940, that I had unorthodox views. I also pointed out that my commanding officer, my fellow-officers and men were well aware of my approach to war — as was the War Office, which had given me permission to contest three by-elections between 1942 and 1944, Winston Churchill's decision that the Atlantic Charter should not apply to Germany having driven me to the hustings. As a contributor to the *New Statesman* had written in April 1944, 'Captain Douglas Home contends that the abandonment of the use of force cannot be achieved by force alone.' Even so, I had been quoted in the press as saying (as indeed I had), 'I will go back to the army, if it should so desire, to fight in a war which I no longer consider just.'

By now, I had been talking for some time, but the court showed no signs of impatience, so I carried on.

I told of how my admiration for the soldiers on both sides on the Second Front increased with every hour, while my contempt for the politicians became more acute.

Testing the court's patience still further, I quoted from a poem I had written a month earlier:

> 'There is no sense in speech, it cannot save us,
> No worth in words, no sunshine in a song.
> We dare not use the gifts our Maker gave us
> Lest we should use them wrong.'

I then came to my peroration on the subject of Le Havre and the refusal by the Allied Commander to allow the evacuation of civilians as requested by the German Commandant.

I closed by quoting Winston Churchill on a previous war: 'Men could not stop because they were caught in the march of events.' It was my contention that men should not be caught in the march of events, but that events should be guided by men.

I then sat down while my friend Major R.W. Edmeades, the commander of HQ Squadron, gave character evidence on my behalf, saying how long he had known me and that he was surprised that a man whose integrity he was there to vouch for should have been brought in front of a military court. He went on to say that he was a regular soldier with no strong opinions on my political outlook, but that he had always found me of good sense and responsibility.

He concluded by saying that he would go perhaps one stage further and say that I had undertaken to the best of my ability anything he had asked me to turn my hand to. The court was then closed for the consideration of the sentence.

In due course I was sentenced to be cashiered and to serve a year in prison with hard labour. When the sentence had been confirmed by Field Marshal Montgomery, I was sent to Wormwood Scrubs and later Wakefield Prison.

Many people, not excluding myself, find it hard to understand why military personnel should be put into civilian prisons. The reason is presumably that, having been cashiered, an officer has ceased to be a military man — unlike non-commissioned soldiery, who undergo their punishment in military establishments.

I found the time — four months were taken off for good conduct — I spent in prison a salutary experience: I learned a lot about my fellow men, and managed to find good in almost all of them.

One comment I would like to make, although it may seem somewhat frivolous, is that the modern furore about 'slopping out' — the early morning emptying of pots down the latrines — was something to look forward to: one could never be sure that one would hit the target, which presented one with quite a challenge each morning.

What is wrong with prisons is that far too many people go to prison who should not be there at all. A bigamist is unlikely to gain any benefit from his imprisonment, apart from the fact that, in a male prison, he will be unable to increase his tally of wives. Nor are those imprisoned for financial double-dealing likely to gain any benefit from their incarceration.

How much better it would be if such people could be dealt with in some other way — through, for instance, monetary or social penalties.

As a result the overcrowding of our prisons would diminish, accommodation would be made available for proper (or improper) criminals, and more chances given to their possible rehabilitation.

Such arguments may seem naive to those who spend a large part of their lives advocating prison reform. Nonetheless, I am convinced that to bring about an improvement in the prison service, the priority must be to reduce drastically the list of crimes for which, at present, prison is assumed to be the only punishment.

The final sentence of my first autobiography, which describes the day I left Wakefield Prison in June 1945, has some bearing on this: 'One or two cameras clicked, one or two reporters asked me what my plans were and then, accompanied by an elderly doctor who had also been released that morning, I walked towards the station down Love Lane.'

I have no inkling of what crime that doctor had committed, nor did I attempt to find out as we walked towards the station, but I am fairly certain that imprisonment in Wakefield was unlikely to have been an appropriate punishment. It would have been better, surely, to have struck him off the Register (which, no doubt, they had done already) and then left it at that: further punishment can only have served to emphasize his degradation and made future prospects of employment in some other sphere less likely.

I had no employment when I came out, and I thought it most unlikely that some impresario would offer me immediate employment on the stage. So I took out my pen and began to write the dialogue of *Now Barabbas* while the memory of prison was still fresh in my mind.

Cynics reading this will no doubt say to themselves 'There you are, you foolish fellow. All your arguments about no benefits coming to prisoners from prison, all your waffling about which crimes should earn imprisonment and which should not, all your pontifications about prison being of no benefit to anyone, are proved to be the nonsense that they are by your own history.' Never, they will argue, has a playwright gained so golden and unique an opportunity as that provided for me by Wormwood Scrubs and Wakefield Prison. Although there may be something in that, I would regard my prison education as a one-off fluke, albeit a rewarding one, and not typical of normal (or abnormal) prison life.

In later life, I met the officer who had been the judge advocate at my court-martial in the Garrick Club. Major Neild (who by then, I think, had become Sir Basil) came up to me in a very friendly manner and asked for a share of the royalties that had accrued to me from the production of my first hit, *Now Barabbas*.

'And what right have you to any share of them?' I asked him.

'Because', he said, with a straight face, 'without my help you would not have gone to prison, and you never would have learned the things that brought success to you and to *Now Barabbas*.'

Then he smiled an impish smile and offered me a drink, which I accepted. Having drunk it, I then offered him the follow-up, which he also accepted; and from that date we became firm friends.

I used to meet him from time to time at prison reform meetings round the country at which we both spoke. In the hotel afterwards, I would sometimes put it to him that, due to personal experience, my speeches might perhaps be marginally better than his. This invariably led to further drinks and increased friendship.

The judge advocate's attitude towards me was typical of most. The majority of people seemed ready to accept that I had acted deliberately, and that such eccentric activity was to be expected of me. Others went so far as to say that my prison sentence was the honourable and inevitable climax to a war spent seeking a nego- tiated peace such as that advocated by those Germans who were involved in the July 1944 Plot against Hitler, whose advances had been rebuffed by those who favoured Unconditional Surrender.

I often talk about these matters with my friend, David Fraser, a retired lieutenant-general and a prolific novelist, as well as the biographer of Alanbrooke. He once told me that the German army's code of military conduct now incorporates the right to disobey an order, whereas the British army still insists that every order has to be obeyed — regardless of an amendment to the Manual of Military Law made in April 1944, of which more anon. Yet at Nuremberg British, French, American and Russian judges saw fit to condemn to death even field-marshals, for the 'crime' of having carried out orders handed to them from above.

Although David Fraser has never gone so far as to condone my offence — indeed on occasion I have heard him deplore it — he regards the situation which prevailed at Nuremberg as a regrettable example of double standards. In his opinion, until such double standards are abandoned by the powers that be, the British military conscience has no right to be described as (or to call itself) clear.

Nor were matters much improved recently by remarks made by our ex-Prime Minister, regarding the Gulf War, in which she threatened war-crime trials and went on to warn Iraqi officers and soldiers that 'the old excuse' (I quote) about obeying orders would no longer apply.

'Since when,' I ask with a cynical smile, 'since when?'

It is hardly surprising that accusations of 'double standards' should be levelled at the British army code, which — or so most people still believe — decrees that enemies should disobey their orders while our own troops should obey them or be punished. It is difficult to see how such consistent inconsistency will ever cease unless the Ministry of Defence adopts a more enlightened stand.

I live in hope that this may happen, even though it is forty-seven years since my own court-martial. As I hinted earlier, my story is not quite over yet: a petition prepared by John Rubinstein, my faithful lawyer, is at present lying on the desk of some high-ranking figure in the Ministry of Defence — or wherever it is that such petitions ultimately end up — the theme of which is that I should be excused, not my imprisonment since I have already served my sentence, but the shame of being cashiered.

To help in this endeavour, John enlisted Colonel Draper, a retired, much crippled officer, who was in no way fit when he agreed to take the task on yet brought his vast experience to bear on my case with tenacity, total application and great courage.

There was nothing in the Manual of Military Law that Colonel Draper did not know about and understand. I use the words 'did not' rather than 'does not' because he died during his investigations. John and I called round to see him once in his flat, where he sat perusing every kind of document, constantly referring to passages in books which he found hard to hold, so crippled was he. I gave him a copy of *Sins of Commission* — a book composed of my wartime letters to my parents, published by Michael Russell — which his widow told me he had read with interest.

One thing that he pointed out to John was that in April 1944 the Manual of Military Law had been amended, making it legitimate for a soldier or an officer to disobey an order which he deemed to be immoral, and excusing him from punishment should it so prove to be.

Evidently the officers presiding over my court-martial were in ignorance of this since throughout the case they emphasized that moral matters should not be allowed to intrude into the discussions, and that their sole function was to prove that the accused had disobeyed a lawful order, never mind its content.

I will end this chapter about war with the last sentence of my speech at my court-martial, paraphrased to tie in with what I remember of it.

'Should I suffer punishment,' I said, 'it will mean that a soldier may not reason why. It will also mean that any officer who thinks like me must either fight or be dishonoured.'

Since I wrote this chapter I have been informed by John Rubinstein that the Ministry of Defence has rejected my appeal.

Ah well, it would have been a turn-up for the books had they accepted it — and there the matter rests at present.

CHAPTER 7

My father stood for Parliament in Berwickshire once when he was a young man. He got beaten by a Liberal, Jack Tennant, by some 7,000 votes — which was about the number by which his third son lost a by-election in England during World War Two, the difference being that as an Independent I lost to a Conservative, since there was a party truce.

From that day on my father gave up politics, which he regarded as an uncertain game to say the least.

When he became the lord lieutenant of his county this stood him in good stead because a lord lieutenant, by the very nature of his calling, should be totally impartial towards any MP or county council of whatever party, Tory, Labour, Liberal or Scottish Nationalist — not that the last of these often feature so near to the English border. Maybe they are frightened of reprisal raids from England by the Percys or the Dacres of the north — although those Dacres fought for James IV at Flodden, while the Dacres of the south were on the English side.

My mother's father, Freddie Lambton, was an MP but, apart from him, there were no politicians in her family or mine; nor had there been for a long time, although some had served as diplomats, one having been ambassador to England with a charming house in Portland Square called Home House.

So when brother Alec, after coming down from Oxford with a third-class honours degree, stood as the Tory candidate for Cathcart, a safe Labour seat in Glasgow, it was quite a novelty. He lost inevitably at the general election, but he cut his teeth on Cathcart to good effect, gaining experience and learning tolerance — not that he ever lacked the latter — as a consequence of his defeat. And shortly afterwards he won South Lanark — in which his Douglas estates are situated — for the Tories, and entered the House of Commons.

From then he never looked back except once, in 1945, after spending most of the War in bed with TB of the spine, he lost his seat in the first post-war general election — a disaster on which my first comedy success, *The Chiltern Hundreds*, was based.

Later on he got the seat back, only to leave the Commons once again in 1951, when he succeeded his father as Lord Home and became a member of the Upper House. And then, by a strange quirk of fate, he found himself back in the Commons as Prime Minister in 1964.

This story is well-known and does not call for repetition here, but it occurs to me that he is not so well-known as a personality as he is as a statesman. This perhaps is due to his undoubted modesty as well as to his tendency to de-dramatize things. In this, it hardly requires saying, he is different from a number of his predecessors.

Indeed, it is likely that, with the possible exception of Lord Melbourne, there has never been a statesman in these islands with such a gift for self-effacement, while at the same time dealing with whatever problems faced him and rendering them harmless.

These inestimable qualities he has put at the service of his fellow-countrymen for over sixty years, and is still doing so in his retirement.

The above may sound embarrassingly like lip-service being paid to a successful statesman by a sycophantic younger brother. That is not the case, however, since I share my mother's independence when it comes to politics — as well as to all else.

She answered, as has often been recorded, the suggestion from a journalist that she must be the proudest mother in the world the day her eldest son became Prime Minister by saying, 'It should have been Mr Butler.' For the record, I do not agree with that assessment and never did, because I always thought that Mr Butler was a trimmer — not that I have very much against such people.

And while on the subject of a subsequent replacement for Sir Alec, I always thought Lord Hailsham far too excitable.

In any case, my mother voted Labour from the day she was enfranchised, up to and beyond the day when her son became Premier — a fact which could perhaps have prejudiced her judgement, had she not possessed such an exceptionally strong character.

The reason that she gave for voting Labour, incidentally, was that although she did not mind Tory policies, she jibbed at their pomposity. And I confess that — as a floating Tory voter — I have sometimes felt like that when Tory ladies (once in mink coats, but not nowadays) have approached me outside polling booths and asked for my voting number. This irritates me so acutely that if they persist, I retaliate by voting left-wing — or as left as I can manage in the Winchester constituency.

Talking of prime ministers reminds me that I edited a book a few years back which covered all the British prime ministers from Walpole to the present day. My favourite was Arthur, Duke of Wellington, whose mother wrote of him at one stage in his life, 'What shall I do with my awkward son, Arthur?'

One evening, a peer came down from Westminster to Apsley House, where the Duke was dining alone. Shown into the presence, and provided with a glass of wine no doubt, he told the Prime Minister that, earlier that night, the Duke of Bedford had made a speech in which he had told the Lords that he would prefer anarchy to what was going on under the Wellington administration.

To which the Prime Minister replied, still chewing his roast beef, 'Go back to the House and tell Johnny Bedford that if we have anarchy, then I'll have Woburn.'

One more story about the great Duke. Doctor Alington, my sister-in-law's father and the then Headmaster of Eton, was dining at the Turf Club with his wife's relation Lionel Ford, then Headmaster of Harrow.

'Cyril,' Lionel Ford said, 'did you know that if the Duke of Wellington's elder brother had done better at Harrow, his younger brother would have followed him there?'

'Really,' said Dr Alington, 'how interesting, Lionel.'

'In which case,' Lionel went on, 'the Battle of Waterloo would have been won on the playing fields of Harrow.'

'Lost, Lionel, lost,' said Dr Alington. 'Let's get on with our dinner, shall we?'

My next hero is Disraeli. He it was who replied to a

questioner who wished to know the difference between a disaster and a tragedy, by saying, 'It would be a disaster if anybody were to push Mr Gladstone into the river and a tragedy if anybody were to pull him out again.'

I like the story too of Mr Gladstone when he was engaged on his Midlothian Campaign. He was working on a speech one winter afternoon, and went for a walk outside Edinburgh. He stopped and leaned on a gate and watched a shepherd driving his sheep out of a valley and up a hill. His task completed, the shepherd came through the gate onto the road, to find himself addressed by Mr Gladstone in the following terms: 'If I were a sheep and the storm were impending, I would much prefer the valley to the hillside.'

'If you were a sheep, man,' the shepherd replied, 'you'd no be such a damned fool.'

So much for prime ministers I've read about. Now for those I have met.

The first I met was Mr Baldwin, who came up to Douglas to address a rally in the 1930s. He and Mrs Baldwin stayed the week-end with my parents and I can recall that Mr Baldwin smoked his pipe when he had finished breakfast at the table at which other members of the family and guests were still engaged in eating.

As befits a pipe-smoker, he was benign and friendly even to the point of saying with a broad smile to my brother Henry, when he came down very late, 'Someone has to be last in this world.'

Mrs Baldwin was benign and friendly as well. I looked at her with awe because I knew that she had played cricket for England when she was young, though I did not dare to raise the subject.

I was also told (by whom I can't recall) that she had made a speech in which she had told her audience that once, while in bed with her husband, she had asked, 'Stanley, do you love England more than you love me?' And he had answered, rolling away (as she picturesquely put it to her utterly astonished audience), 'Yes, Lucy, I believe I do.'

One Prime Minister I did not meet was Neville Chamberlain,

although Sir Alec had worked for him as his Parliamentary Private Secretary before and during the war, until he was stricken with TB.

Nor was I present, being in London, when he asked his boss and his wife up to Hirsel after Munich to stay with my parents. The arrangement was that they would come to Hirsel for a few days and then go to Birmingham to stay with Neville's sister on their way back down to London. They arrived with Alec, and my parents got on very well with them and vice versa.

After a week had elapsed, however, my father remarked to Alec, 'I like poor old Neville and his wife, but when the devil are they leaving?'

'When they go to stay with Neville's sister down in Birmingham,' said Alec.

'So I gathered,' said my father, 'but when?'

'When they get a letter from her,' Alec answered, 'but it hasn't come yet.'

'I see,' said my father, somewhat restlessly.

That night Neville's sister rang to ask when they were coming. 'When you ask them,' Alec told her.

'But I wrote last week,' she said.

'Well, it's not come yet,' Alec answered.

She fixed their visit for the following day, and next morning they departed.

'Dear old people,' said my father, as he waved them off. 'Thank goodness his sister rang up. Otherwise they might have stayed for ever. Wonder why her letter never came?'

'Yes, so do I,' said Alec.

Some days later, he was flighting some pigeons. Taking out a cartridge from his jacket pocket to re-load, his hand came up against a stiffish piece of paper which turned out to be an envelope addressed to Mrs Neville Chamberlain. It was the letter everybody had been waiting for.

When Alec came in for tea he confessed this to my father, who laughed and said, 'Well, it's lucky I kicked up a dust in that case.'

Poor old Neville Chamberlain — he did his best and no one can do more than that. And one is glad to note that understanding of his policy and the necessity of playing for time at that stage is increasing as the years go by, allowing a more calm appraisal of the situation to be made.

The next Prime Minister I met was Winston Churchill, who came down to Eastwell Park in 1944 to inspect our new tanks. My colonel, Roscoe Reid, being a charming if somewhat mischievous man, detailed me to show him my troop, which consisted of three Churchill tanks. The fact that I had only just returned from losing my deposit at a by-election in Clay Cross, which I had fought against the Coalition Government, did not seem to worry Colonel Reid. In fact, I think it amused him. Whether the PM knew anything about this or had caught my name when I was introduced to him, I can't be sure.

What I do know is that the Colonel, for reasons best known to himself, assumed that I disliked my main political opponent personally — whereas, in truth, I much admired him, though deploring his addiction to the policy of Unconditional Surrender — and that he sat beside me in the carrier which took us to the tank park, with the PM, in his sawn-off top-hat, sitting opposite us. As we rattled down towards my troop of tanks, the Colonel whispered to me, 'I'd ask you to hand over your revolver, if I didn't know it was too dirty to loose off!'

That leads me on to other memories of him as told me by other people, notably my brother Alec.

One of them describes how, as a member of a shooting party, the young Winston, then in his teens, was walking through the park at Blenheim in line, when a hare got up some way ahead. He fired with both barrels, but missed it.

The keeper next to him rebuked him, telling him 'That hare was far too far away to shoot at, Master Winston.'

Master Winston disagreed. 'I wished that animal to know it had a part to play in our proceedings,' he informed the keeper.

Then there is the tale told by Sir Alec of a farewell dinner at Buckingham Palace, given by the King for the heads of the American armed services at the end of the War before they returned home.

Over coffee, the King's Secretary spotted a US naval officer slipping a gold spoon into the pocket of his mess kit as a souvenir. The Secretary went over to Sir Winston to inform him of the fact, and said that he thought that he should tell the guests of what he had seen in order to prevent a lot more coffee spoons from disappearing.

'Don't do any such thing,' Mr Churchill said. 'Leave it to me.' At that he put a gold spoon into the breast pocket of his tail-coat, sticking out an inch or two, walked round the table to the culprit and said, 'We've been spotted — we'll have to give them back.'

Poor Mr Churchill, as he still was then — the victor of the greatest war in history, and so soon to be removed from office by his fellow-countrymen and women. How must he have felt after Labour's landslide victory that July? Thrown aside? Unwanted? Possibly. Or just the victim of an overwhelming longing for change? I would guess the last, since magnanimity, even towards himself, was one of his most admirable qualities. Another was his impish sense of humour, which reduced most things to size.

Not long before the 1945 election, my brother Alec was summoned by the great man and told that he was being sent to Edinburgh as Under Secretary of State for Scotland in the last days of the Coalition Government.

As he reached the door on his way out, he heard his leader say, 'And go and quell those bloody Scots and don't come back until you've done it.' Looking back he saw the PM's visage wreathed in smiles behind the smoke from his cigar.

A great friend of Winston Churchill, whom I never met, was F.E. Smith, later Lord Birkenhead. He made a speech in Liverpool one night — or rather he failed to make it, even though he had been called upon to do so.

The Lord Mayor, or some such dignitary, spoke for half an hour or more by way of introduction. F.E. grew more and more impatient since he had a train to catch; so when the speaker ended his prolonged oration with the words, 'I now ask Mr F.E. Smith to give us his address,' the great man rose to his feet and, folding up his notes, said, 'My address, my Lord Mayor, is 3, Grosvenor Square, London' (or whatever number it was) and then left the platform en route for the railway station.

Another story, which occurred after his elevation to the House of Lords, concerns the Atheneum Club.

He used to lunch well in the Upper House, with almost certainly a glass of wine or two. After making a speech, he would walk home through Green Park and up the Duke of York's Steps — at which point he would almost always want to relieve nature, for which purpose he would call in at the Atheneum.

This incensed the members, somewhat understandably, since he was not a member of the club. One day, after the hall porter had reported that Lord Birkenhead was downstairs in the lavatory again, the Club Committee placed a bishop in the hall to intercept him on his way up.

'Excuse me, Lord Birkenhead,' the bishop said, when he appeared, 'are you a member of this club?'

'So it's a club too, is it?' said Lord Birkenhead, and went on his way.

The next Prime Minister I met was 'Uncle Harold' Macmillan — nicknamed thus by many, like myself, who bear no relationship to him (or very little).

One of my favourite memories of him is the occasion on which he sat down after an eve-of-poll speech, in Stockton-on-Tees, from which north-eastern town he ultimately took his title. Up got a miner, thanked him for his speech, and then went on to ask him why he thought that a miner should consider voting for him. Did he not appreciate the fact, the miner went on, speaking passionately, that miners and their families used outside toilets at the bottom of the garden all the year round and in every kind of weather, because indoor plumbing was denied to them and, in so far as he could forecast, always would be?

He sat down to great applause, after which 'Uncle Harold' rose to answer him. 'You have my sympathy,' he said, 'and you will understand precisely why you have it, when I tell you that when I first married Lady Dorothy there was only one lavatory in Chatsworth.'

He then sat down, while his audience asked themselves if they were not, perhaps, much better off with one earth closet in the garden than the family at Chatsworth had been in the not far distant past, with their staff and guests relying on one water-closet. And if Chatsworth had been modernized, might there not be some hope for them as well!

The first time I met 'Uncle Harold' was when he came up to shoot at Douglas with Sir Alec. After dinner over the port,

Alec having left the room to talk to someone on the telephone, he turned to me and said, 'Did you ever meet Lloyd George?'

'No, sir,' I answered.

'He had very small feet, you know,' Uncle Harold told me. 'He should never have gone into politics, he should have been a ballet dancer.'

On Alec's return, he turned to other subjects.

I heard him make a speech once at a dinner given for John Betjeman, and was surprised by how closely he held his sheaf of notes to his eyes. After dinner, I asked somebody who had been sitting near him at the top table how he managed to read anything at all at such close range.

'He didn't have to,' my informant told me, 'there was nothing written on those bits of paper. They were just for show!'

There is a story told about a drinks party. In his later years he indulged his tendency to shuffle in his walk — a ploy he used when he wished to strike a sympathetic chord in the hearts of his guests at Birch Grove, thus ensuring that they would not forget a brave old widower, doing his best to entertain them.

Having bade the last guest farewell after the party, or so the story goes, he came back onto the lawn where his grandchildren were starting to play croquet, to be told by one of them, 'You can walk properly now, Grandpa.'

What an actor Uncle Harold was — and would have been had his road through life led him to the stage rather than politics.

His wife from Chatsworth (Lady Dorothy) stuck to him, though her liaison with Lord Boothby did not make life any easier for Uncle Harold. She was an outspoken lady, and it's said that, coming up from London to attend her brother's funeral at Chatsworth, she found herself in a queue on the platform at Chesterfield Station waiting to hand her ticket in. As her luggage passed by on a porter's truck, she shouted to her daughter further up the queue, 'Sarah, you bloody fool, you've forgotten the Scrabble.'

Other Prime Ministers, apart from Alec, whom I met albeit briefly, are Ted Heath, Lords Callaghan and Wilson and once, at lunch, Mrs Thatcher.

I have little record of the first three except that I was once responsible for filling Harold Wilson's pipe.

It happened in a Birmingham hotel, where we were both

engaged to make a speech at some literary lunch. When I arrived I saw him pacing impatiently up and down the lounge and asked him what was troubling him. He told me that he had no tobacco left in his pouch, so I filled him up from mine. It held a brand called Seventh Reserve, which I had bought in Perth in Scotland. Harold Wilson liked it so much that he asked me for the source from whence it came. The next time that I was passing through Perth I called in to enquire at the tobacconist's if they had signed up a new customer called Harold Wilson. They shook my hand benignly and conceded that they had just done that very thing.

The only time I met Mrs Thatcher was at a luncheon given for Sir Alec's 'eightieth' at Chequers.

Although I hardly spoke to her, she was a very friendly hostess and we had a very happy visit, made more memorable by something that her husband said to Rachel at the luncheon table, where she had been seated beside him.

I have heard it said that private conversations should not be recounted in print, but I look upon myself as being totally excused from any such stricture because Mr Thatcher's comments could be heard around the table, much to the amusement of the other guests.

We had arrived at the front door by a lane that twisted its way through some farm buildings, but when Rachel sat down, she saw through the window of the dining-room a long drive — not unlike the LongWalk in Windsor Park — stretching through the park into the distance.

'When you come here, Mr Thatcher,' she enquired, 'do you come by the little twisty drive we used, or by the long one?'

His reply was this: 'I drive down every Friday night behind the Boss and mean to use the long one, but the buggers always shut the gate in my face, so I have to come round by yours.'

Memories of my brother Alec as Prime Minister are not extensive because he did not stay in office very long.

My favourite concerns the famous occasion at the United Nations when Mr Khrushchev waved his shoe round his head and then beat the podium with it.

I asked Sir Alec, who was present, if this action had surprised him.

'No, not in the least,' he told me, 'as I had been watching him undoing his shoe-laces!'

I like his tales about Gromyko as well. On one occasion my brother asked his Russian counterpart up to shoot at Douglas.

'Is it on private land?' Gromyko asked him.

'Yes, of course,' said Alec.

'Then I cannot come,' Gromyko said.

'Not even', countered Alec, 'if I hand it over to the county council for the day?'

'Not even then,' smiled back Gromyko.

So he never went to Douglas, but he did shoot when on holiday in Russia on the Black Sea.

This Alec found out when, dining out with their wives in a London restaurant, Gromyko asked him for advice about the purchase of two pairs of sporting guns in London.

'Do you want the best?' asked Alec.

'One pair better than the other pair,' Gromyko answered.

'Will your government be paying for them?' Alec asked, knowing that Mr Khrushchev owned a pair of Purdeys.

'Who knows?' said Gromyko. At this point, my brother mentioned Purdey and some other gun-makers, and then asked who the two pairs were to be for.

'Myself and my son,' Gromyko answered.

'And who's going to have the best pair?' asked Elizabeth, across the table, of Mrs Gromyko.

'I think it is better that our son should have the best pair,' said she, 'as unlike his father, he allows the ducks to rise from the water before he shoots.' Nor did her husband dissent from that view.

There was a rumour at the time that Mrs Gromyko found Sir Alec much to her taste. Whether this was true or not, I am in no position to assess. All I know is that once, when Alec and Elizabeth arrived at Moscow Airport, Mr Gromyko shook hands with them both, then, turning to Elizabeth, remarked, 'My wife will not be pleased to learn that you are here with your husband.'

Gromyko had a twisted smile which much appealed to me, and leads me to suppose that he was not without a sense of humour. Nor did he lack common sense. How else did he survive in Russian politics for so long — just as Talleyrand did under not dissimilar circumstances?

To get back to Sir Alec, it is common knowledge that he stood down after losing the 1964 general election. Yet he only lost by a handful of seats, which was astonishing considering that he had taken over from Uncle Harold a dying government beset with scandal; it may well be that under a different leader the Conservatives would have lost by possibly a hundred or even two hundred seats. Nor was he helped by the defection of MacLeod and Powell at the start of his administration — indeed this may have tipped the scales with the electorate.

In any case, it was a noble effort, worthy of the highest praise — as was his readiness to serve under Ted Heath after the Tories resumed power in 1970. Though not a staunch Conservative, I find it hard to criticize his ministerial career in any way. It seems to me to be a blue-print for a politician of whatever party.

Now, at eighty-seven, he has virtually left politics, although he still speaks in the Lords on a variety of subjects — or did before he had his stroke — always succinctly and sensibly, and with a touch of very welcome wit.

The last speech that I heard him make was to the Winchester School Political Society, when he spoke for just under an hour on Russia, past and present, and the prospects for the future of that country and its erstwhile satellites. He answered questions for another half-hour and then carried on discussions with the boys around him during dinner, with the chaplain in charge of proceedings. And he did all this even though his back, never the soundest part of his anatomy, was hurting him.

His imperturbability has always been his strength, whether laid up in bed during the middle of the War or, as a politician, dealing with tolerance and understanding not only with the problems facing his own country, but with those facing others, whether friends, enemies or ex-colonials. And his sense of humour remained intact always, enabling him to defuse any awkward situation.

I recall the story of his being photographed with Humphrey Gibbs shortly after sanctions had been imposed on Rhodesia. Seated on the lawn beside the Governor, the Foreign Secretary was heard to say, 'Well, sanctions don't seem to be doing much harm to your roses, Humphrey.'

One overseas Premier I met at luncheon with Sir Alec one week-end at Dorney Wood, where ministers were wont to entertain visiting statesmen, was Sir Robert Menzies. Alec, I remember, asked Sir Robert why, if he was the true Scot he always claimed to be, he pronounced his surname 'Menzys' rather than 'Mingys', as preferred by all those of that name in Scotland.

'Interesting question, Alec,' smiled Sir Robert. 'I'll look into it when I get hume!'

CHAPTER 8

One other claim to fame I have as far as politics are concerned is that I knew a President of the United States before he got that far, and for too short a time thereafter.

I first met him through his sister Kick or Kathleen, an amusing girl of great attraction and vitality, when I went round to take her out to dinner from the US Embassy — a year or two before the War. I was waiting for Kick in the downstairs sitting-room when a man appeared in white tie and tails, bearing a tray with drinks thereon, which he placed on a table.

Thinking that he was the butler, I politely asked if I could have a small whisky and water.

'I guess you could if you could pour it out,' he said. He was, of course, no butler but Ambassador Joe Kennedy, on his way out to dinner with some notable.

When Kick came down, she laughed when I told her of my adventure.

Later, at some dance or other, of which there were plenty in those pre-war days, I met her sister, Eunice — a delightful and outspoken girl — and Joe and Jack, her brothers. And sometimes in the Embassy garden on a summer evening, I would see Bobby and an even smaller Teddy bicycling around the lawn. I did not meet Jean until later, as she was the youngest.

Joe was a delightful young man but more serious than Jack, who was the male equivalent of Kick, his sister, in that he was always ready for a cheeky remark and a joke.

Joe, alas, was killed in the War in the air force, and Jack nearly died as well in the Pacific when his ship went down. For the rest of his life he had a bad back, which gave him much pain.

I was an actor at the time, while Jack was at the London School of Economics under Harold Laski.

One day we played a game of golf at a course just outside London. Although it took place over fifty years ago, I recall that game with total clarity because when, in the pro's shop, we both asked a young man there for four or five new golf balls, he handed us each a box containing a dozen Dunlop golf balls, saying as he did so, 'Take the lot. We're giving them away this morning.'

Off we went in some bewilderment to play our round, occasionally remarking on how philanthropically we had been treated, though we could not understand why.

On our return, we learned from a small group of golfers gathered outside the pro's shop that the young assistant who had treated us had been removed by men in white coats just in time to stop him emptying the shop entirely. Whether we gave back our boxes of Dunlops, I cannot now recall.

In 1939, a week before the War broke out, I dined with all the Kennedys near Cannes. We listened to Lord Halifax's gloomy broadcast after dinner, and then I returned to England by train with an Englishman, called Brian Johnston, who was trying his French out on his fellow-passengers.

Before long all the Kennedys had returned home, though Kick came back to marry Billy Hartington, who was killed shortly afterwards. She stayed in England and I met her one night when she asked me to a brains trust at a US service club in Kensington. I noticed then how bravely she was taking her loss.

When I was in Wakefield Prison, she came to visit me, showing me all her old friendship and affection, and after my release in 1945 she asked me to many drinks parties to help me rehabilitate myself.

One of these took place on an evening when I had been summoned to a meeting chaired by Ethel Manning, at which I had been expected to declare myself an opposition candidate in the ensuing general election to a Tory by the name of Winston Churchill.

But, as I informed my hostess and her guests (one of whom was Lady Dorothy Macmillan), I had just decided not to stand against him in the interests of a serving private soldier who had recently announced his candidature, as I did not wish to split the independent vote.

When the election came along, believe it or not, a last-minute entrant got 10,000 votes. Sometimes in the watches of the night I still wake up and think to myself that — given how unpopular he was at that stage, as the general election so astonishingly showed — I might have beaten Winston Churchill, my old war antagonist. Yet, had I won — as I announced in my election address, which I had already written — I would have stood down at once in order to allow my adversary to regain his seat at the ensuing by-election.

Thus, I figured, I would teach him and the country a sharp lesson — though the latter, as it turned out, did not need it.

So, instead of going straight back into politics, I went north to the Borders for a rest. This did not last long, because soon after I got there I sat down and wrote the two plays that, two years later, proved to be my first theatrical successes. The first was *Now Barabbas* — a drama set in prison — and the second was *The Chiltern Hundreds* based on the 1945 general election in which Alec lost his seat.

Jack came back to London in 1946 or 1947, I forget which. He looked well, despite the cortisone for his war wounds. Both Rachel and I liked Jackie the first time we met her.

He did not discuss my war career, though he often joked about it in a friendly manner. I found him as cheerful and observant as he had been before the War.

One summer, in the early Fifties, we stayed with Jack and Jackie at the Villa L'Horizon, an exotic mansion they had taken from the Aga Khan just east of Cannes.

I remember sitting in the garden after breakfast with Jack, looking seaward at a motor boat that was careering through the waves towards the landing-stage, driven by a dashing young Italian who had arranged a little water-skiing between the islands.

'That guy isn't coming here to pick up you and me,' said Jack. And sure enough, he planned to go water-skiing with our wives — a plan that was fulfilled after my first attempt at water-skiing had ended with me under water, with my water-skis against the bottom of the boat.

Thereafter we indulged in more peaceful pursuits on Eden Rock.

I well remember lying on a raft with Jack and Michael Canfield, his brother-in-law. Also with us, as I recall, was David Tomlinson, the actor.

In my waking dreams, I heard the voice of Michael saying, 'Jack, I just can't understand why you want to be President.' A short silence ensued, and then Jack said, 'Well, Mike, I guess it's just about the only thing I can do!'

The last time I saw Jack's father was when we went to lunch with him near Cannes sur Mer, in a villa that he took each summer. As we drove up the drive, with what seemed to be a footman under every palm tree bowing to us on the roadside, Jack said, 'I see that Dad's roughing it again this year.'

His quips were endless. In the Casino one night an American lady told him that she did not like to see a future President of the United States playing roulette, and he thanked her for the prophecy but not for the rebuke.

We met in the United States a few years later, first in New York when he came to the first night of *The Reluctant Debutante*, and then when we stayed with him in Washington en route for Hollywood.

The last time that we met him was in London, after he had become President. He was returning from a trip to Russia to see Mr Khrushchev, and had made his speech beside the Berlin Wall. He came for drinks with Jackie's sister, Lee Radziwill. He was the same as ever, cracking jokes with all and sundry, with that familiar twinkle in the eye.

Then one week-end Aidan Crawley and his wife came to see us, and as they arrived they told us of the tragic news from Dallas.

I sat down, wrote four lines of verse and sent them to the *Evening Standard*. They printed them next day in their earlier editions:

> 'There, in a sun-kissed street in Dallas filled
> With cheering crowds he died and at his end
> The heart-beat of humanity was stilled
> To mark the passing of a faithful friend.'

He would have laughed at it, of course, if he had been alive to read it, just as he had laughed about an exhortation I had sent him once during some crisis — an extract from my play *The Thistle and The Rose*, which ran as follows: 'There never was a situation in the world so warlike or so dangerous, but cool and level-headed statesmen could control it, if they willed to do so in their hearts. I pray you to be temperate.'

Well, laugh or not, that is what he turned out to be during the Cuban Crisis!

My favourite British politician, though she never reached the highest office since in those days such a situation had not been envisaged (except possibly by her!), was Lady Astor, at whose home at Cliveden the young Kennedys were always welcome.

My first meeting with her occurred when I was at Eton. The natural history society had an outing in the park at Cliveden, and we were invited to take tea thereafter on the terrace.

I clearly remember Lady Astor coming out of the house, walking over to our table and examining each one of us with an amused and penetrating gaze. She then turned to the master-in-charge and remarked, 'Well, what else can you expect? But my conscience is clear, because I never stopped tellin' their parents not to marry!'

There was a short silence followed by much laughter, and I loved her from that moment.

The stories told about her are, of course, unending. Most of them are true, however — such as the remark she made to Mr Lee, her butler (only recently deceased), when he came in to tell her he was leaving after many years of service.

'Tell me where you're goin', Lee,' she said, 'because I'm comin' with you.'

Quite unable to resist her ladyship, he stayed on for many years.

He was a splendid man, was Mr Lee — as friendly to young strangers as he was to royalty and statesmen, and perhaps more understanding. For example, knowing his mistress to be strongly anti-drink, he hid a glass of whisky among the flowers in the drawing-room, hoping it would satiate the thirst of those young men (like Michael, her third Astor son) who did not share her view.

Michael and Jakie, his younger brother, often asked me down to Cliveden for the week-end in those pre-war days. As a result, I got to know their mother very well.

Her maiden name was Langhorne and she came from Virginia, as everybody knows. One of her sisters married Rachel's great-uncle Bob, as already mentioned. Yet another married Dana Gibson, a fine artist. When I told my mother this, she said, 'Ah, that explains why I have always thought that Lady Astor was a Gibson Girl.'

I reported this remark to Lady Astor when I met her next. 'Silly old woman,' she said, 'sittin' up there in Scotland drinkin' tea and knowin' nothin' about anythin'.' Not true, of course, but Lady Astor liked to answer back, and what she liked to do, she always did.

I played golf with her once at Burnham Beeches during the War, after arriving there from Devonshire where I was stationed in a dungeon called Fort Scraesdon, built to keep Napoleon at bay. Washing facilities were not exactly lavish in that area, but not as bad as Lady Astor thought they were, judging from her remark when she first introduced me to my caddie. 'Don't go too near him,' she said. 'He hasn't had a bath since war broke out.' In spite of this beginning, or perhaps because of it, all four of us enjoyed the round immensely.

Michael and Jakie were my best friends. Michael was a merry fellow, and became an MP when the war was over. His political ambition, so he told me, was not office, but to put a ferret into the red box from which the Chancellor produced his speech on Budget Day.

He never managed to fulfil this ambition, however, and after some years he became disillusioned with the life that he had chosen as a handy substitute for war. On one occasion, his constituency association failed to find him when they wanted him, and sent an urgent message of complaint to both the House of Commons and to his home. His answer came back next day from somewhere overseas, in a telegram which read as follows: 'You must take me as you find me, if you can find me.'

Later he resigned his seat and went to Bruern Abbey, his delightful home in Gloucestershire, where he became a country squire. He painted in his spare time, profiting no doubt from the painting lessons he had in Northern France when he was in the Phantom Reconnaissance Regiment, the headquarters of which was in Regent's Park.

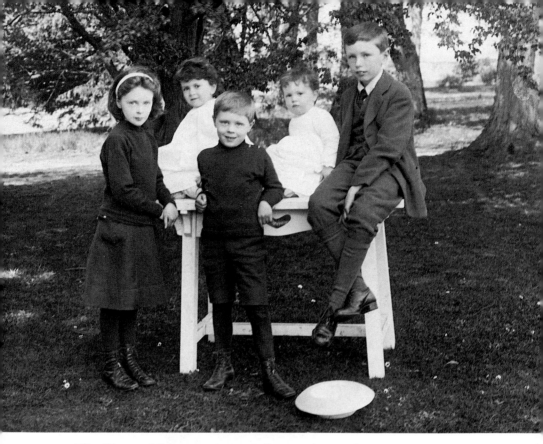

The Home children in 1914. Left to right: Bridget, Rachel, Henry, myself and Alec.

My mother.

Above: *Shooting with Johnny Dalkeith at Douglas.*
Below: *Off to a lecture at* Oxford. *Left to right: Mark Pilkington, myself, Charles Wood and Brian Johnston as groom.*

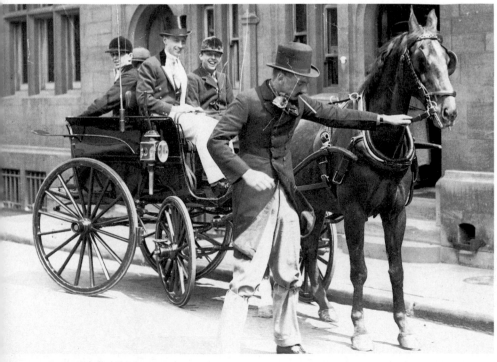

Opposite: *Fishing for salmon with my father on the Tweed.*

Above: *With Jack Kennedy at the Eden Roc, Antibes, 1960.*

Below: *My lifelong friends Michael (left) and Jakie Astor. The former was my best man.*

Opposite: *Rachel and I were married at St Peters, Eaton Square.*

Clockwise from top left: *Ralph Richardson; Rachel with Jack Merivale; myself with Wilfrid Hyde White; Celia Johnson; Anna Massey.*

MARGARETTA SCOTT RAI[...]

Change of
sex, a
dangerous
subject?
not on your
life, as created
by William
Douglas Home
and played by
Henry Kendall
...is good
for laughs
as deep as I
have had for
a long time

[...]NT EDWINA

A New Comedy by WILLIAM DOUGLAS HOME

[...]MARASCHAL   **KENNETH FORTESCUE**

NICHOLAS SELBY   PETER CELLIER   HILARY TINDALL

DOROTHY BAIRD   MARINA MARTIN

DIRECTED BY WALLACE DOUGLAS

Settings by MICHAEL WEIGHT

Above: Aunt Edwina *at the Fortune Theatre in London.*
Below: *Appearing with A. E. Matthews on* This is Your Life.

Above: *My nephew Charlie Douglas Home, then editor of* The Times.
Below: *Brian Johnston with his goddaughter, and my daughter, Dinah.*

His job was to take his scout car and his driver to brigade headquarters and try to glean information from staff officers, either through conversation or through their wireless networks which would cast light on the progress of the War. This he would relay back to Regent's Park via the wireless in his scout car, in the hope that he might have turned up something worthwhile.

One day he was passing through a village on his way to brigade headquarters when he saw a board outside a house informing all those who passed by that painting lessons were available at a price from the householder, who was quite a well-known artist. Michael booked himself in for a few days, leaving his driver in charge of the wireless link with Regent's Park.

As I have said before, Michael was my best man at my wedding. As we stood waiting for the bride, who turned up late due to a traffic jam, he whispered to me, 'It's like waiting for pigeons — they always turn up in the end.'

He died young, leaving behind a large number of friends who knew in their hearts that they would be extremely lucky if they ever met a more endearing character, however long they might survive him.

Jakie served in another section of the Phantom Regiment, and found himself parachuted into Southern France during the Second Front. Like Michael, he became a Tory MP when his mother finally stood down in Plymouth.

He was a popular MP who, like his mother and his brother before him, saw the funny side of things. One morning a constituent came to his 'surgery' (so-called, though I've never known exactly why) and, presumably to save a stamp, handed him a letter addressed to his gardener's wife, which he delivered faithfully.

He much enjoyed his speech-making in Plymouth, though he never provoked such a classic retaliation as his mother had when, in the course of a speech, she told her audience that she would rather commit adultery than drink a glass of beer — at which a naval voice from the back of the town hall shouted 'Who wouldn't?'

Jakie reacted strongly to the Suez crisis, and was totally convinced that the whole project was a great mistake. The Chief Whip at that time was Edward Heath, to whom he wrote apologizing for what could have been construed by narrow-minded people as disloyalty; Heath informed him that he much respected him for sticking to his point of view. From then on, like Michael before him, he became less interested in active politics.

He now lives with his third wife, a charming lady and a sculptress of ability. Although he suffers from Parkinson's Disease, he still plays golf, so well is his affliction kept under control. I hope that what occurred the last time we played together will occur again, because the memory still makes me laugh at frequent intervals.

Arriving at the golf club, Jakie said to me, 'I only play nine holes as I'm a sick man. So don't be a bloody fool, and try to make me play more.'

'But I wouldn't dream of it,' I told him.

'Good,' he said. 'Well, don't forget it.'

Off we went, with Jakie playing well and myself, strange to relate, even better.

I was one up after playing eight. On the ninth tee, I stooped to stick my tee into the ground, and, as I did so, Jakie looked up at the sky and said, 'It really is a lovely day. Let's go on a bit, shall we?'

'All right,' I said, hiding my smile, and then drove off.

Four or five holes later — after he had safely beaten me — he said, 'We'll stop now, shall we, as you must be getting tired.'

His mother would have liked that story!

At Brancaster once I asked him to move his feet because they were between me and the hole. 'Why not go round them?' he suggested. He won't mind me writing things like that about him. Every Astor, as I have implied, says what he (or she) wishes to. And I am glad to say that I have never met an Astor who did not concede that privilege to others.

May he go on playing golf for many years to come, for never mind who wins (and he invariably does in my experience), one finds oneself opposed by a unique and charming adversary.

Now back to his mother, Nancy, and her first reaction to Waldorf, his father.

After the break-up of her first marriage, she arrived in England for the hunting season. She met Waldorf Astor, and her first comment was 'I love Waldorf, he's so rich.'

Apart from that undoubted fact, he was a man of great integrity and breadth of vision. He was also patient with his wife and family, regarding both his wife and younger sons as lovable eccentrics and greeting all their boisterous outspokenness with a benign smile.

Once, on his way back from the Derby, his car stopped beside a taxi in a traffic jam. In it his youngest son Jakie was seated, a cigar in his mouth, heading for Eton, from which he had taken the day off without permission. Waldorf let his wife deal with the delinquent through the open window of the Rolls-Royce — as a result of which Jakie, who had avoided quite a few off-duty Eton masters at the races, began to wish that he had met them rather than his mother.

Only once did Lord Astor himself take action against his youngest son, and that was when the two of them were listening to the radio news one night in Jura, where they were on holiday. From it they learned the tragic news that a quartet of Eton masters (Slater, Powell, Howson and Whyte-Thomson) had all perished from a fall while climbing in the Alps.

'I bet it was Slater's fault,' Jakie remarked, half to himself. At this his father sent him out onto the hill, nor did he let him in again until the early hours.

Mention of Eton brings to mind the occasion when Lady Astor came to see her sons at Eton on the Fourth of June, during Jakie's first year there. She went to Mr Huson's house, where Jakie boarded, and informed him that she wished to see his room. 'But it's right at the top of the house,' Jakie said, anticipating possible embarrassments ahead, should his mother be in an outspoken mood.

Sure enough, as they approached the top floor, down the staircase came the Captain of the house, a most distinguished character in Pop, with seals in his top-hat, a coloured waistcoat and patent leather shoes — the kind of character of whom all new boys stood in automatic awe.

Poor Jakie cowered underneath the bannisters to let him pass. But not so his mother.

As he went by, she put out a hand and seized him by the shoulder. As he twisted round to look at her, she turned his head back with her other hand; and then, after a short pause for inspection, she remarked, 'Thought so. Dirty ears, just like your father.' After which she let him go and walked on up the stairs, with Jakie following behind like a crushed beetle, so appalled was he by her behaviour.

There was a happy postscript to that tale, however. Jakie told me that the Captain of the house did not attempt to pay the son back for the mother's tactlessness. Instead, he seemed to feel that the poor little creature needed his protection from then on! And yet her tactlessness concealed a heart of gold, and all my memories of her are of her kindness.

When I got married she gave me a bed and some silver for a wedding present. I wrote back to tell her how delighted I was, and reported that the bed was large enough for three — and would she come and stay the week-end with us. Back came an open postcard saying 'Thanks for the invitation, but Her Ladyship prefers to sleep alone.'

After Lord Astor died, she moved into a flat in Eaton Square. One visit Rachel and I made to her there sticks in my mind. Rachel's uncle, Bob Brand, was also present; and as we sat over tea she suddenly pointed at him and said, 'This old man's waitin' to marry me, but I'm not havin' it.' Bob winked at us, and then held his tea-cup out for a refill.

The day came when even her lively and indomitable spirit weakened. Jakie went to see her in her bedroom on her birthday. She looked up at him and said, 'What are you doin' here?'

'I've come to see you, Mama,' Jakie told her.

'Because it's my birthday? Or because I'm dyin'?' she asked.

'Well, a bit of both,' he answered gently.

Her eyes twinkled and she laughed aloud.

There were those who criticized her for her outspokenness and tactlessness; such as when she told Winston Churchill that, if she was married to him, she would put poison in his coffee — to which he replied, 'I'd drink it, if you did.'

But, in general, she was much loved for her beauty, her transparent honesty, her wit and, above all, her kindness. Unfathomable goodness was her outstanding contribution to this world — a quality in which she was as rich as Waldorf was in dollars.

Among other politicians I have warmed to in my time were

Jock MacEwen and Bill Anstruther-Gray — MPs in succession
for my father's county of Berwickshire.

Jock was a broad-minded Tory whose family consisted of one
daughter and five sons. It was a pleasure in the post-war years to
go to Marchmont, up the road from Hirsel towards Edinburgh,
to meet this happy family.

His wife, Brigid, was the daughter of the diplomat Sir Francis
Lindley. She told me once how she had been first drawn to Jock
when he was an attaché at her father's embassy in Japan.

One afternoon, the family went down to swim and Jock, the
new attaché, asked Miss Brigid if she would consider giving him
a swimming lesson.

Since she was intrigued by him, they went into the sea together
where she taught him how to do the breast-stroke, exhorting him
to keep his legs and feet up rather than allow them to trail low.

Back home at the embassy, she found that she had left her
hand-bag on the beach, and went back to retrieve it.

As she came in sight of the beach, she observed far out to sea
a figure swimming fast and furiously — which, when it returned
to shore, turned out to be none other than the young man she
had been instructing earlier.

From that moment, she decided that a man with a mind so
adroit as to enable him to think up such a scheme, however
superficially deceitful, would be well worth marrying.

This diagnosis proved to be correct, for they lived happily
for many years thereafter.

When Jock finally became a Roman Catholic — a faith his
wife had always followed — he gave up his seat in Parliament,
and was succeeded by Bill Anstruther-Gray.

Bill was married to my cousin Monica. Her father, Geoffrey
Lambton, was my mother's brother, and was killed in the First
World War.

Bill was a sterling character — a stolid, solid, bluff and hearty
fellow, with a most endearing grunt which sounded like 'hum-yep'
and punctuated almost every sentence that he ever spoke. It also
added emphasis to everything he said, although whatever he said
scarcely needed emphasizing, since it seemed emphatic enough as
it was.

A good example of his attitude to life occurred at a public

meeting in the town hall in Coldstream. My brother Henry went to it, and immediately reported back to me.

A questioner got up and said 'I saw that you voted in the House of Commons last week against capital punishment.'

'That's right,' said Bill, 'hum-yep.'

'But, if I may say so,' said the questioner, 'you don't look to be the kind of man who would.'

'Then I'll tell you why I did,' said Bill, 'hum-yep.'

'I would be grateful,' said the questioner.

Bill rose and spoke as follows. 'During the war I came back from North Africa on leave. I didn't ring my wife from London when I got there as I wasn't sure what train I'd catch to Edinburgh. And when I got to Edinburgh I didn't ring her either, as it was too early in the morning. So I took a taxi to Kilmany and arrived there about 7.30 and went up to see her in her bedroom. Well, if there'd been a man in bed with her, I would have shot him stone dead. Hum-yep. And I wouldn't have deserved to die for that.'

Then he sat down to great applause, during which Monica whispered to Henry, 'Lucky that he didn't come the night before!' (A joke, of course.)

I had a bet once in a shooting-brake, en route to shoot at Tullybeagles with George Lansdowne and John Nelson. We were going to meet Bill at Bankfoot and take him on from there, and we bet on whether he would say 'What fun' during the drive of two or three miles.

Those who had their cash on silence looked increasingly pleased with themselves as we approached our destination. The car stopped and out we all got, stepping into a torrential rain-storm mixed with hail. Bill looked up at the sky and said 'What fun! Hum-yep,' and some of us collected.

After he was elevated to the House of Lords, Bill did wonders saving the salmon in the North Sea from excessive seine-netting.

Three other ex-MPs for whom I have a great respect are Sir Charles Mott-Radcliffe, Jo Grimond and Johnny Dalkeith.

Grimond has become a member of the House of Lords, as has Dalkeith under his new title of Buccleuch; Sir Charles retired some years ago from Windsor, which, as I have already recorded, he won during the War in a by-election fought under the party truce against myself, fighting as an Independent, which indeed I was.

Charlie Mott-Radcliffe had been in my house at Eton, so we were old friends, though locked in mortal conflict fighting a by-election in our military uniforms.

We never had an angry word to say to one another throughout the long three weeks during which we campaigned in the Maidenhead and Windsor areas. When we parted after polling day, he having beaten me by 2,500 votes or so, we shook hands, totally exhausted, and returned to our respective regiments.

I met him at the Eton celebrations in 1990 and reminded him of the two telegrams — one for each of us — which arrived from Cairo during the count, both of them from Neil Heneage, then in Egypt serving as a colonel. He had been in our house at school, in which we had all been tended by Miss Owen, our delightful dame, or matron. Whenever we found it hard to swallow some dish served up during house meals, she invariably said to us with a benign and deprecating smile, 'Remember that there's always ham.' Which tale explains the texts of the two telegrams that we received that morning, which read 'Good luck, and don't forget that never mind which of you wins the election there is always ham.'

Another missive I had from Neil came from the War Office, to which he had been transferred in 1944. It read, 'How are you? Or have I already sent you to your death with a stroke of my pen?'

Jo Grimond, who was also in our house, succeeded me as house captain after I left. I sometimes wonder if Miss Owen realized that she was nurturing a nest of politicians under her wing.

Benign as ever, and as lively as he was when he was at school, Jo does not need reminding when we meet (although I invariably do so) of the day when I lunched with him in the New Club during a by-election in South Edinburgh which he had talked me into fighting as a Liberal.

As we began our meal, I asked him, 'Jo, at all my meetings from tonight on, for the next three weeks or so, what is the key theme that I should be plugging on about?'

'Proportional representation,' he said. He then took a sip of wine, put down his glass, and said with feeling, 'Wouldn't it be awful if we ever got it!'

Full of personality and blessed with great broad-mindedness, Jo knows how to treat dogma, never mind how sacred it may be, with a smile and a pinch of salt.

Now for Johnny Dalkeith, the last of a most personable trio.

At the general election in which I fought South Edinburgh as a Liberal, Johnny was standing for a nearby seat — which, incidentally, he won for the Tories.

A year or two later, I received an invitation to attend a meeting of the Roxburgh and Selkirk Liberal Association in the Station Hotel in St Boswells, so that I might be assessed as a potential candidate.

On the morning of the date in question, Johnny rang us up and asked us both to dinner at Eildon nearby St Boswells.

'We'd have to have it early,' I replied, 'as I have a meeting somewhere in your area at eight.'

I did not mention where or what about, since he was in the enemy camp.

'Splendid,' he replied, 'we'll have it at quarter to seven.'

We arrived and sat down to a sumptuous supper, with food and drink provided on a princely scale.

At ten to eight, I rose — although I found it fairly hard to do so steadily — and drove off to the Station Hotel.

I forgot to mention that I was dressed in a velvet smoking jacket which Johnny had suggested that I wear for the dinner.

I was ushered into a small room in which an enormous fire was burning — as far as I remember it was mid-May — placed in a chair beside it, and then subjected to cross-examination.

After a few minutes, I began to break out in a muck sweat, caused by the wine I had drunk at dinner and by the closeness of the room, in which about a dozen people were sitting in a temperature beyond endurance — my endurance anyway.

The meeting ended as soon as I could make it.

I returned to Eildon to be comforted by Johnny with a glass of whisky. He, of course, had known about the meeting all the time, the cunning fellow, and had arranged the dinner and the smoking jacket and the hospitality so as to ensure that I should make a bad impression, which — since I was not selected — must have been the case.

I laugh about that episode still. And I sometimes wonder

whether David Steel should not be grateful to both Johnny and myself for ridding him of a potential rival for the seat he later represented for so long.

CHAPTER 9

S o much for politicians. I now propose to write about another calling somewhat similar to theirs in that it, too, is prone to constant change and fluctuating fortunes, with success an ever-present goal that, in most cases, is only intermittently achieved: that of the actor.

I was one myself for a few years before the War — a sojourn at RADA was followed by a stint in repertory, then two plays in the West End.

That I did not continue as an actor after 1939 I tend to put down to the intervention of the War — but in fact I have a sneaking feeling that, had it not intervened, I might have found myself a little short of parts. I was not at all that bad, although light comedy was all that I aspired to: I was unsuited to tragedy because of my dead-pan face, or perhaps because of my voice and natural ability.

Although I performed for three weeks in the Theatre Royal, Windsor, in *The Young Idea* by Noel Coward, I spent more time before I was called up in July 1940 in writing plays than I did in acting — which convinces me that, had war been averted, I would still have left the stage and taken up the pen instead.

But that is a subject I mean to tackle later on. In the meantime I intend to write about the many actors I have got to know during my fifty years and more in the theatre, most of whom have acted in my plays which is the reason why I got to know them.

The first actor of note I met was Sir John Gielgud (then plain John) on whom I pressed a play of mine called *Great Possessions* while he was having coffee in the Caledonian Hotel in Edinburgh, during a tour of *Richard of Bordeaux* in 1935 or 1936.

Somewhat surprised, he took it — and, what's more, he read it and wrote to say that he had sent it on to Stephen Haggard, a young actor whom I much admired at that time. He also read and enjoyed it, but not quite enough to want to act in it.

The trouble that those two went to, and the kindness they showed me, encouraged me no end just when I needed it most. Since that meeting with Sir John over fifty years ago, I've made a point of seeing all the plays and films that he has acted in and gained a lot of pleasure from them all.

Great Possessions was produced while I was still at Oxford and then ran in the West End for about six weeks. I then wrote another, *Passing By*, while I was waiting for my call-up papers, which came on in 1940 for a season at the Q Theatre in Brentford. Thereafter my theatrical career came to a halt until the War and my imprisonment were over, when I sat down and wrote a play about the latter, *Now Barabbas*, which turned out to be my first success.

The leading man in this play was a friend of mine called Richard Longman — brother of the publisher Mark — with whom I had lunch in London soon after my release from prison. He and Raymond Westwell, who had been in my regiment, arranged for it to be presented at the Boltons Theatre in Kensington, which had just opened with John Wyse as the manager and Colin Chandler as the chief director.

The cast of *Now Barabbas* also included Percy Walsh, an actor I had much admired in *French Without Tears* in pre-war days. He played the warden who looked after Richard Longman in the condemned cell.

Both of them — and indeed the whole cast — were outstandingly good, as was the direction, and in due course it arrived in London at the Vaudeville Theatre, to the plaudits of the critics.

The actor whom I got to know best in the early post-war years was A.E. Matthews, who played the leading part in my first comedy success, *The Chiltern Hundreds*, in 1947 and which replaced *Now Barabbas* at the Vaudeville Theatre at the end of the former's run.

Matty, as he was known, was very old, but as lively as a cricket. When some cheeky young reporter rang him up and asked him how he managed to continue acting at his great age, he said, 'It's quite easy, my boy. I read the obituary column in *The Times* every morning at breakfast, and, if my name's not in it, I go to the theatre in the evening.'

An indomitable character, he lived in Bushey Heath near Watford with a younger wife (his second, or perhaps his third). He had a habit of remarking as he left the stage at the conclusion of a scene, 'Where am I off to now?' 'Your dressing-room,' some helpful colleague on stage with him would reply in an aside, for which Matty would thank him and shake his hand as he went off.

I have heard people say that he forgot or paraphrased his lines. This is not so. In fact he learned and said them to perfection. I say this from experience and with conviction, since the rhythms that I write in never suffered the least damage when spoken by Matty.

He was perfect in *The Chiltern Hundreds* and equally as good, though in his mid-eighties, in its sequel, *The Manor of Northstead*. He sometimes forgot himself, but never his lines. For example, when up in Glasgow on tour after the London run was over, he went to lunch with a whisky merchant — with the result that he did not perform in the ensuing matinée, which he slept through in comfort in his dressing-room.

Charles Hislop, who was playing Beecham — the co-starring butler in the play — seems at the time to have understudied Matty. How this came about, I've never understood, unless the proper understudy was off playing golf on the assumption that old Matty, who had never let him down, would not do so that afternoon. But the fact remains that Charles somehow contrived to perform his own part while, at the same time improvising the lines of his delinquent colleague.

The *on dit* was that he did it very cleverly, but I am glad to say I was neither present at the matinée nor at the performance that night, after Matty came to.

That, I think, was probably the only time that Matty failed to make it in his lifetime, though there had been minor grounds for worry during the play's run in London — which led Peter 'Mousetrap' Saunders, who had produced it at the Duchess Theatre, to ban drink in the dressing-rooms.

One evening, some weeks later, Peter went to call on Matty in his dressing-room to discuss something before curtain rise, only to find that the door of his dressing-room was locked.

He knocked and Matty opened it, let him in and invited

him to have a drink. Before Peter could answer, Matty had plucked a gin bottle from underneath a make-up towel. As he poured the drinks, he said, 'I have to do that as that bugger Saunders, who put on this play, won't let us have drinks in our dressing-rooms for reasons best known to himself.' As he raised his glass, he looked up and recognized his visitor.

Charles Hislop, as I have said, played the butler in *The Manor of Northstead*, whereas Michael Shepley played him in *The Chiltern Hundreds* itself. He was a robust, outspoken character. In his dressing-room one night, after I had gone round to tell him how good his performance was, he told me that he was going to propose me for membership of the Garrick Club. I thanked him for the kind thought and went my way.

Months passed, and then one night I went to see him again to pass the time of day (or rather, night). He greeted me and offered me a drink which I accepted — as one did in those days, before breathalizing had changed the face of the world.

As we raised our glasses to each other, Michael told me that he had changed his mind about the Garrick and decided not to put me up because, on second thoughts, he had decided that I would be black-balled — due no doubt, although he did not say so, to the fact that two years earlier I had been in the Scrubs.

I told him not to worry, and that I was sure that his decision was wise. Incidentally, another twenty or thirty years passed before some bold adventurer saw fit to put me up again — successfully so.

The Garrick Club, if I may be permitted to divert from my main theme just for a moment, is a splendid institution filled with judges, lawyers, impresarios, writers and actors, not to mention broadcasters and the occasional aristocrat or country squire. Maybe it harbours bishops as well, though I do not recall seeing one.

But, strange to say, it lacks theatrical agents, one of the most potent forces in the theatre, without whose services many members of the Garrick would be on the rocks.

I found this out when I asked Laurence Evans of the ICM why it was that I never saw him there. He told me he was not a member because those who practised his profession were not usually welcome in the club as members.

I asked why and he told me that the reason for the ban was because the committee thought agents would talk business to their clients on club premises, and thus destroy the anti-business discussion atmosphere prevailing in the club — in their imagination, at least!

I add that rider since the fact is that in every club (from the Ark onwards) business between members is always on the menu, be they politicians or clergymen, members of the Jockey Club or of the armed services.

Although I've never raised the subject with the club committee, I have a strong feeling that a pipe-dream of that nature ought to be abandoned since it never could be realized, as anyone who has lunch in the large dining-room (as well as in the small one) and is not deaf will confirm. The ban on agents like my friend Laurence Evans is not only totally unfair, but laughable as well.

A dinner was held in the Garrick, which alas I could not go to, to celebrate the hundredth birthday of Athene Seyler, who died recently aged 101. I had seen her in the club a week or two before and found her looking just as lively as she had looked in my play *The Iron Duchess*, thirty-odd years earlier.

The story goes that when the love of her life, a former actor called 'Beau' Hannon, fell in love with her he made arrangements to divorce his wife, as the result of which he ended up in Brighton in a hotel with some lady of convenience for the night.

When his case came up in court, all went well until the hotel maid was called into the witness box. When asked the routine question, 'Did you see this gentleman in bed with this young lady when you took in their breakfast?' she answered 'No.' Nor, never mind how hard they questioned her, would she be moved — for, having fallen for 'Beau' Hannon when she saw him in bed, she decided not to get him into trouble, never mind how hard she had to lie.

She succeeded all too well: though nobly (if mistakenly) conceived, her persistence prevented him from getting the divorce he was seeking.

Another story about this happy pair concerns a time when they stayed together at the Imperial Hotel in Torquay.

One evening, Athene finished dressing and went down to

have a drink in the bar before dinner. Time slipped by, so she went up in the lift to hurry up her 'Beau'. She walked along the corridor, opened a bedroom door and saw a figure with its back to her, clad only in a shirt, the buttons of which he was doing up in front of the mirror. Moving forward quietly, she came up behind the gentleman, took him firmly by the genitalia and sang out, 'Dingle, dangle, dinner's ready.'

To her utter consternation, when he turned he revealed himself to be a bishop whom she had seen down in the lounge at teatime.

She retired in much confusion to the bar downstairs, where 'Beau' was by now having an aperitif, and told him of the trouble she had got herself into as a result of leaving the lift at the wrong floor. One assumes — although I have no confirmation of the fact — that they decided to go out to dinner that night, rather than encounter an embarrassed bishop in the hotel dining-room.

Her co-star in *The Iron Duchess* was Ronald Squire, a man of infinite charm and an actor of immense ability in comedy. I doubt if he tried tragedy at any stage in his career, but, if he did, I reckon that the twinkle in his eye, the creases in his cheeks and the benign and gentle smile that accompanied everything he said would have precluded him from gaining stardom in that field.

Nor, I guess, would he have wished to. For him life was a gentle and amusing affair, and the slings and arrows of outrageous fortune were most definitely not the stuff that Ronnie would have wished to demonstrate in action.

He had an appealing daughter, Jacqueline, to whom I was engaged for a short period when I was in a play with her and Ronald and Yvonne Arnaud. She went off to Hollywood before the War. I have not seen her since although she wrote to me, God bless her, to commiserate about my sojourn in the Scrubs in 1944-5.

In the mid-Fifties Paul Clift — an old impresario of great charm — put on *The Reluctant Debutante*, directed by Jack Minster and starring Wilfrid Hyde White and Celia Johnson. The name-part was played by a girl called Anna Massey, who had never previously been on stage.

She had done recitations at the evening parties that her

mother, Adrienne Allen, gave for her theatrical friends, but she had not been to acting school or voice production classes. She must either have been a natural, or Jack Minster had turned her into a professional during rehearsals. Anyway, she came up trumps, as did Jack Merrivale and Peter Myers, the two young men, Anna Steele, the second debutante, and Ambrosine Philpotts, who played the friend of the family.

Even Jack Minster seemed delighted with it (I say 'even' because Jack was always hard to please) as were the critics, except for Peter Ustinov, who said it was 'a fall from grace on the part of the author of *Now Barabbas*.' I took this criticism with a pinch of salt, however, as I knew he must be standing in for some critic on holiday.

But in general, *The Reluctant Debutante's* reception could not have been better, although 'Jolly Jack' (as Minster was nicknamed throughout the theatre) could never quite shake off his pessimistic outlook.

To give an example of this: one night he was rung up at home in Windsor from the Cambridge Theatre by his company manager.

'Good news tonight, Mr Minster,' said he.

'Oh, yes?' grunted Jack.

'The Queen Mother's in the stalls with a party of six,' the manager went on, 'and Princess Margaret's in the circle with a party of eight.'

Silence reigned for a time. 'Did you hear me, Mr Minster?' asked the manager.

'Yes,' a sepulchral voice replied, 'I did.'

'Then why don't you sound more pleased?' asked the manager.

'Because the Queen's the only one who really counts,' said Jack, as he hung up.

Wilfrid Hyde White was a joy to watch in the part of the father, Jimmy Broadbent. He had precisely the right blend of cynicism and concern for a daughter launched into that strange bazaar devoted to the art of matchmaking.

I played the role myself for two weeks after Wilfrid had a minor motor accident. According to his version of events, he had hired a car constructed of Ryvita (a kind of toast) which sustained a knock when someone stopped in front of it too quickly. Shaken by the impact, he retired to bed in Hampstead where he lodged with his friend, Ballard Berkeley.

I went up to see him one day to find his bedside table covered with full and empty champagne bottles. He was looking very well but told me that, in his view, he had earned a rest and meant to be bedridden for at least three weeks.

The next time I went to see him he was raring to come back. The reason for this change of outlook was that he had received my first week's box office returns — which revealed, to his horror, that the takings during his first week in bed had been larger than those of the week before. The takings during his second week away were even larger, due to the fact that the Motor Show, which invariably led to major bookings, coincided with his absence. He was unaware of this; nor did I enlighten him, since I wanted him to think that his replacement had exceeded him in popularity!

At any rate he came hurriedly back next week — and, to his delight, he found the takings were even higher.

I enjoyed my sojourn in the part, although my first night proved a nerve-racking experience — which ended happily, however.

I was removing my make-up after the curtain-call when the call-boy came to say that Celia would like to see me in her dressing-room. I went along the corridor in trepidation, thinking she was going to say that I was too bad to continue in the role, and that performances would have to be suspended until Wilfrid came back.

I found her sitting in front of the looking-glass removing her own make-up. As I came in, she offered me a drink. I took it — she had one already — after which she turned and looked at me with those enchantingly wide eyes of hers and said, 'Would you mind putting milk into my coffee in the breakfast scene in the last act in future, as I can't sleep if I drink black coffee at night.'

Celia was being as practical as ever — just as she was when she suggested to Paul Clift at a casting session that Jack Merrivale should play the part of the young man.

'Is he a good actor?' Paul asked.

'I wouldn't know about that,' Celia replied, 'but he can drop me off on Henley Bridge each night on his way home.'

Later, *The Reluctant Debutante* was turned into a film by Metro-Goldwyn-Meyer. The leads in the film were Rex Harrison, Kay Kendall and Angela Lansbury, playing the part Ambrosine Philpotts had performed so beautifully in the play. An American girl, Sandra Dee, played the debutante and an American boy, John Saxon, her future husband.

This strange casting came about because the play had been adapted by the Americans for Walter Pigeon, who was then not free to act in it. Rex was then asked, who said he did not like the revised script and wanted me to put it back as it was.

The end result worked well enough, though it was not entirely unconfusing since Kay Kendall had to be a step-mother in order to account for the Americans in the cast.

Now Rex is dead, and so is Celia. One misses them acutely, and remembers them with gratitude.

The last production that Jack Minster did for me was called *A Friend in Need*. Its stars were David Tomlinson and David Hutchinson. During rehearsals, Jack muttered his best-known line. 'Don't look at the floor,' he advised one of the actors, 'because you'll see that the play's lying there', his favourite comment always being 'Lift it off the floor.'

It had a minor run in London, but did wonders in South Africa when David Tomlinson took it out there. David has been off stage for some years now, but I would like to see him in revivals of such plays of mine as *Lloyd George Knew My Father*, *The Kingfisher* and *After the Ball is Over*, which was once put on by the Compass Company with its founder, Tony Quayle, playing the lead: it did not receive the notices it deserved from those dramatic critics who disliked its theme of fox-hunting.

Another actor I admired tremendously was Kenneth More. When the producer John Gale told me that we would have to wait a year to sign him for *The Secretary Bird* I was perfectly happy to do so, since I knew that he would act Hugh Walford to perfection — as, indeed, he did.

He was a charming actor with a ready sense of humour and, at the same time, an undercurrent of emotion which, while suitably suppressed, was nonetheless apparent.

In his dealings with a wife who wanted to run away with a much-married younger man, he was the epitome of gentleness, while at the same time displaying a quiet determination to retain her by whatever means available.

The play ran at the Savoy between 1968 and 1971; Kenny was succeeded by John Gregson, and later by Jeremy Hawke.

Some years later, Ralph Richardson and Peggy Ashcroft came to the Savoy in *Lloyd George Knew My Father*, a play which had first seen the light when performed by Eton boys directed by Tom Wheare, now the Headmaster of Bryanston, who had telephoned me to ask if I had an unpublished play available.

Ralph and Peggy were a charming pair.

I have used that word 'charm' a great deal when describing the actors I have dealt with in my life. The fact remains that an actor needs a lot of that commodity, especially in comedy, if he (or she) is to enchant playgoers. Tragedy, of course, requires another quality, namely sincerity.

It was once said, I think — by whom I can't recall, perhaps it was myself! — that an actor should be sincere in his insincerity. This does not, however, mean that actors should be insincere in character — only that actors should assume the mantle of their necessary insincerity, then be sincere in putting it across.

The combination of Ralph Richardson and Peggy Ashcroft in *Lloyd George Knew My Father* gave me intense pleasure. Never, in my recollection, did I ever meet a more eccentric man. He had a mischievous smile which suggested that he was well aware of the effect his eccentricity had on his friends and colleagues, and enjoyed that knowledge to the full.

His wife Muriel, better known as Mu (who performed in *Lloyd George Knew My Father* with him in Australia), once told me that she was looking out of the window of their house in Regent's Park one day and saw him revving up his motor-bike.

'Where are you going, Ralph?' she called.

'To see my rat in hospital,' he called back as he rode off.

His pet rat had been left with the vet as the result of some mishap or other. Back he came in due course with his friend, now restored to health, in a box on the pillion. He told me once that in his experience, rats were without doubt the nicest pets of all. I took his word for it, but was not tempted to test his claim.

I once asked him to lunch at the Travellers' Club. When I arrived the hall porter informed me that Sir Ralph was waiting for me — which became immediately obvious when I entered the hall and saw his crash-helmet among all the bowlers and Anthony Edens hanging in the hat-rails.

After lunch he told me, in the smoking-room, that I should write a play that he had had in mind for ages, called *The Bloodstained Mouse*.

'And what would be the plot?' I asked him.

'This,' he said. 'The setting would be a smoking-room in a club such as this. The oldest member is asleep in his chair after lunch. Beside him on the floor is a copy of *The Times*, which has slipped off his knee. On its uppermost page can be seen the blood-stained footprints of a mouse, which appear to lead back to a cupboard door, set in the wall close by.'

'Go on,' I said.

'No — you go on,' said Ralph. 'You are the playwright.'

I must confess that I have never yet got round to doing so. One day I may try to, when I can think of nothing else to write about.

One night when we were on tour with *Lloyd George* on its pre-London run, I saw Ralph off from the Grand Theatre in Leeds after the play was over.

'Where are you staying, Ralph?' I asked him as he got into his car.

'The Harwood Arms,' he told me.

'Do you know the way?' I enquired.

'Not entirely. But the car does,' he replied, patting the dashboard with affection as he drove tentatively away.

During the War he and his good friend Laurence Olivier were pilots in the Fleet Air Arm. The story goes that they seldom returned to base in one piece — or if they did, then their aeroplanes did not. As far as Ralph was concerned, it seems that he sometimes forgot his bearings (and/or his map), with the result that he landed not on the runway from which he had taken off, but in a cornfield or a meadow, the bumpy surface of which tended to damage his wheels and undercarriage.

Indeed, I have heard it said that the new project at the Old Vic — which was started during the War with Olivier and Richardson in charge, and later became the National — was favoured by their previous employers as a welcome means of saving money by permanently grounding two intrepid if absent-minded pilots.

Ralph enjoyed the National when it was finally built, though he had one minor criticism of it. Rachel and I once went to see him in his dressing-room after an evening spent at *No Man's Land*. We congratulated him on his performance, and after downing the drinks that he had provided — or, in my case, downing half of it and, with the assistance of his understanding dresser, pouring the other half down the sink — prepared to take our leave of him.

'Hold on,' we heard him say. 'You mustn't go alone.'

He donned his dressing-gown and joined us in the corridor.

'It's quite impossible to get out of this place alive,' he went on, 'unless you're in the secret. So let me conduct you to the stage-door, or they'll find your skeletons in some damned cupboard a few weeks from now.'

With that, he led the way through endless corridors until at last the stage-door hove in sight. We thanked him for escorting us and stepped through it — looking back to see a smiling figure waving at us.

Celia had taken over in *Lloyd George Knew My Father* after Peggy had fulfilled her contract. Ralph was initially put out by this change of leading lady, complaining that Celia had, when passing him his coffee cup, presented it to a different hand than Peggy.

This acute dilemma was resolved to everybody's satisfaction at the next performance, whether due to Celia's surrender or to a minor adjustment to his own performance by Ralph.

From then on, he warmed to his new partner. Only when she too left at the conclusion of her contract did Ralph reckon he had had enough of playing General Sir William Boothroyd in the West End.

When Ralph went with Mu, first to Australia, and then

to Canada and Washington, he was replaced by a dear old friend of mine, a kilted Andrew Cruickshank.

The last play of mine in which Ralph appeared was *The Kingfisher*, produced in London in 1977, once again with Celia. The only other character was played by Alan Webb. The first night was bedevilled by a power cut, which postponed the opening for two hours. Nonetheless, the critics were mostly favourable — barring Bernard Levin, who had retired for some years as a drama critic and was standing in for someone else. He was as vitriolic towards me as he had been so often in his youth.

'Would that some persuasive spectre had warned Celia Johnson and Ralph Richardson against appearing in *The Kingfisher*,' he wrote in the *Sunday Times*. 'Such a waste of talents, I have rarely seen. Little plot, less wit and no point.'

As is so often the case in the theatre, I did not see enough of Ralph once *The Kingfisher* had come off after a good run. This does not mean that the friendships made with actors are just bread-and-butter affairs. On the contrary — they are firm and readily renewable at any time.

But since dramatists and actors tend to be involved in other plays, once the production that united them has dropped its final curtain, new friends temporarily replace the old ones until there is a further opportunity for a reunion.

Ralph died, alas, before such a reunion could take place. The word went round that his last words were spoken to Mu after he had looked at her, silently and intensely, as she sat by his bed. 'That's some hat,' he said.

Rachel and I attended his memorial service in the Abbey. There was not an empty seat, and there was a large crowd outside: which proved — if proof were needed, which it wasn't — that not only a great man had passed that way, but also a much-loved one.

CHAPTER 10

I only once met Sir Ralph's great friend, Laurence Olivier, and that was in St Martin's-in-the-Fields, at Celia Johnson's memorial service.

Rachel and I were in the front pew, and he came and sat beside us. The clergyman in charge approached and whispered to each of us in turn. 'You, Lord Olivier,' he said, 'will use the microphone beside the altar steps when you read your piece.' Then he turned to me and said, 'You, Mr Home, as you are giving the address, will climb into the pulpit.' Then he went to meet the family at the church door.

Olivier leaned over to me, looked up at the pulpit and said, 'Watch out that I don't upstage you and go up there for my bit first.'

What a man he was. No actor in the history of the British stage had such charisma. Not even Sir John Gielgud, his great rival and perhaps a marginally better actor, could compete with him in that sphere. Never mind what part he played, or in what media, he dominated all his fellow-actors with his voice, his personality and his technique — except, perhaps, for a pre-war *Romeo and Juliet* in which he and Gielgud alternated as Mercutio and Romeo. My own view was that whereas Olivier was more swashbuckling as Mercutio, Gielgud was more moving as Romeo. But to try to assess which of them earned more marks would be a fruitless exercise.

Sir Laurence was a great experimenter on stage. Sir Ralph told me that he once appeared with him in *Othello* in Canada, playing Iago to Sir Laurence's Othello. Much to his horror, he was kissed full on the lips by the Moor at a rehearsal.

He rebuked Sir Laurence to some tune, only to be informed that he intended to do the same thing on the first night.

'Then you'll have to get another fellow,' Sir Ralph spluttered, shivering his timbers.

'Calm down, Ralphie,' said Sir Laurence, 'and just listen to me, will you.'

Then he launched into a long description of how he had met some erudite professor who had spent a lifetime studying the Bard and had informed him that Othello was enamoured of Iago, and that were such a relationship to be established on stage, the play would become more realistic and effective than ever before.

'So, Ralphie,' he concluded, 'don't be such a sissy.'

'Sissy, me, I like that!' spluttered Sir Ralph.

'Well then, spoilsport,' said Sir Laurence.

Came the dress rehearsal, and Sir Laurence did it again. Up Sir Ralph rose from his couch in a blind fury, turned to the director who was sitting in the empty stalls and shouted, 'I'm not acting with this crazy pouf! You can get someone else.' He then stamped off to his dressing-room. They calmed him down, of course, and he agreed to continue on the understanding that, if Sir Laurence tried it on again, he would react with equal violence and thus wreck the ending of the play — though by then, to everyone's relief, Sir Laurence had conceded defeat and thus saved their friendship.

Other actors I have enjoyed working with are Derek Nimmo, John Mills, Michael Denison and Dulcie Gray.

In Derek Nimmo, I have found a champion not only at the Shaftesbury, where he revived *A Friend Indeed* for a season in the mid-Eighties, but overseas as well.

For many years now, he has taken companies to Hong Kong, Singapore, the Gulf and many other places and he has been kind enough to take a few of my plays, such as *Lloyd George Knew My Father, The Reluctant Debutante, The Secretary Bird, The Kingfisher*, etc.

Moira Lister played the lead in *The Reluctant Debutante*, and judging by the Hong Kong notices and Derek Nimmo's report she gave a great performance. She became ill and, after playing bravely on until the close of the Hong Kong date, came home for an operation, from which she has made a good recovery. She was replaced by Barbara Murray, who flew out to only ten days of rehearsal.

The Kingfisher starred John MacCallum, Googie Withers and the late-lamented Gordon Watson. This too was a great success and the reception that those three got every night was well-deserved.

Googie and John have always been friends. Googie is a splendid and indomitable lady as well as a versatile performer. John plays golf far too well to suit me. He makes the perfect leading man, especially when opposite his wife; their partnership has endured for many years, both on and off the stage. In short, they are two enchanting people, well loved both Down Under (John is an Australian) and in this country.

One incident involving John that tickled me occurred when he was in *The Baccarat Scandal* by Royce Royston, a play about Sir William Gordon Cummings which I saw at Chichester. John played a general who was a week-end guest at Tranby Cross at the same time as the Prince of Wales (later King Edward VII).

He and the actor playing the Prince were both called on to give evidence after Sir Gordon Cummings had been accused of cheating at baccarat.

After giving his evidence, John went and sat on a chair upstage. The Prince gave his next, then joined John and sat down beside him. After a few minutes, I saw John get up and slip out through the wings. He never came back. When we saw him in his dressing-room at curtain fall, I asked him whether he had been taken short and, if so, whether he was feeling better.

'What the devil are you talking about?' he asked.

'Well, you left the stage after your evidence,' I said, 'and never came back.'

'What was the point of staying,' said he, with a twinkle in his eye. 'I had no more lines!'

John Mills, Michael Denison and Dulcie Gray were in a play of mine, *The End of the Day*, produced in the West End in 1973, in which John played Harold Wilson, Dulcie Gray played Mary Wilson and Michael played Ted Heath. It did well and was performed enchantingly by all three of them — proving, beyond doubt, that plays about well-known politicians need not be performed by comic look-alikes but rather by good actors, acting with sincerity.

John Mills looks younger every day, while Michael Denison and Dulcie Gray never change. I saw them a few years ago in *The Kingfisher*, with Bobby Fleming playing the third part. All three performed it charmingly.

Another actor I admire is Tony Britton, who appeared in *The Dame of Sark* with Celia, playing the part of a German colonel, Count von Schmettau. I was impressed by all the trouble he took to make sure his interpretation was authentic, even going so far as to call up Count von Schmettau's son in Germany and asking him about his father's mannerisms and his style of talking English.

Although *The Dame of Sark* is one of my plays that I like best, my favourite is (and always will be) *The Queen's Highland Servant* which is about Queen Victoria and John Brown. It first opened in Salisbury in 1967 under the direction of Oliver Gordon there, the following year in Windsor directed by Hugh Goldie with Pamela Stanley in the leading role. Before the War, I had seen her play the Queen in Lytton Strachey's play *Victoria Regina*.

After Windsor it transferred to the Savoy for a short season, filling in a gap between productions caused by some play unexpectedly and prematurely failing — as plays often do!

It was revived some years later for a season at Pitlochry, where I thoroughly enjoyed it once again. The actress playing the old Queen was excellent, and I remember asking the director in the interval why she had never reached the heights in her profession. 'Because she is only twenty-one,' he told me. I forget her name, but I am never likely to forget her acting and would like to think that she might get in touch with me if she ever reads this.

That play fulfilled to perfection the necessary requirements for a good play — good and varied parts, a strong plot and an unforgettable denouement. Writing it required intense research — a thoroughly enthralling exercise, which sometimes came up with rich rewards, such as the story about Lady Ely, one of the Queen's ladies, and her mistress.

They were driving in the Isle of Wight one afternoon after Prince Albert's death. The Queen was looking sad, and Lady Ely, hoping to persuade her to give up pining for her Albert, as she had been doing for some years, much to the disappointment of her subjects, said, 'Cheer up, Ma'am, I know that when we die we will all meet our loved ones in Abraham's bosom.' To which the Queen replied, 'Jane, I will not meet Abraham.'

Another actor whom I would have liked to see more of was

Tony Quayle. I met him first when he was asked to do *Rolls-Hyphen-Royce*, a play of mine about the birth of that great car firm. I remember him requiring alterations which I thought well beyond the call of duty, so that first encounter was a brief one. The play came on some years later: it encountered stiff opposition from the critics and did not survive long. Nonetheless, I still regard it as a favourite of mine which should be revived one day.

One reason for its poor reception was, in my view, Wilfrid Hyde White's strange performance as Claude Johnson, the go-between between Charles Rolls and Henry Royce, the former played by Peter Egan, the latter by Alfred Marks.

As always, my heart was in my mouth at curtain-rise. By the time Wilfrid's first speech had ended, it was in my boots.

The opening speech that I had provided for him as an introduction to the play ran as follows:

Good evening, my name is Claude Johnson, C.J. to my friends. I'd be surprised if more than ten per cent of you have ever heard of me. But, nonetheless, I was quite well-known in my hey-day. Someone even wrote a book about me once but they didn't call it either C.J. or Claude Johnson, they called it *The Hyphen in Rolls Royce*. Hence the name of this play.

I'm not the leading character, far from it. Henry Royce is that, of course, and Charles Rolls is the second lead by virtue of the fact that he dies prematurely, just before the interval. I'm just the commentator or the chorus or the hyphen since, as I've already indicated, it was me who brought the two together.

Instead of saying this, which would have set the play moving on the right lines, Wilfrid started off quite differently.

He walked down to the footlights and said words to this effect: "Allo, it's nice to see you. Wish I knew just how you got here, what with all these one-way streets. And now you're here, I doubt if you'll get away for the same reason. So, see you again tomorrow.'

Not content with that, which left me sweating through my shirt, he then looked up at the roof above the auditorium and added solemnly, 'And, by the way, I don't know if you know it, but that roof fell in a few months ago. Watch out that it doesn't do it again tonight.'

He then started out on the lines quoted earlier — but by now every ounce of atmosphere had been destroyed, and the audience was nervous and bewildered. As John Peter said in his *Sunday Times* review, 'This is not a stage actor. It is a Hyde Whitor.'

It took some time for Alfred Marks, Peter Egan and the rest of the cast to re-establish any atmosphere at all — and then Wilfrid destroyed it all over again when he remarked to Peter Egan in a front-of-curtain scene, 'I'd ask you to sit down, but I'm afraid they've only set one chair.'

'Old rascal' is the phrase that I would use to describe Wilfrid's irresponsible behaviour that night, and that is what I called him after curtain-fall, with suitable embellishments. But he never apologized, nor did he regret for one moment what he genuinely thought had been a charming introduction, well designed to get the audience on his side at least — if not the play's!

That was the last time I saw Wilfrid acting — or rather 'performing' — until last year when Jack Merrivale, a week or so before he died, rang up to say, 'Switch on your television tonight and, believe it or not, you'll see Uncle Wilfrid in a spaceship.'

Sure enough, I turned it on as bidden and saw Wilfrid doing a live programme with a lot of spacemen dressed in spacesuits. He, needless to say, was in his usual greatcoat.

What it was all about I have no idea — only a nostalgic memory of Uncle Wilfrid's voice haranguing his companions on some subject, the purport of which escaped me.

Wilfrid, alas, is now dead but I shall always treasure his memory and the endless stories about him.

Always nervous of his health, Wilfrid took every necessary precaution to avoid chills. I recall him coming to stay once for the racing at Goodwood. While we were playing croquet one sunlit evening, I looked up at Wilfrid's bedroom window and, to my surprise, I saw that his curtains were drawn. Wondering if he was ill, I hurried upstairs to check up, and found him in bed in his greatcoat with the electric fire full on.

'Are you ill, Wilfrid?' I asked.

'No, my boy, just resting, that's all,' he replied.

'Well, come and have a game of croquet, or you'll give yourself heat-stroke,' I said. Up he got and joined us on the croquet lawn, still in the greatcoat.

He drove down from London for that visit and reported that there had been a bad traffic jam near Guildford.

'Bad luck, Wilfrid,' I said, as I carried in his suitcase.

'Actually, it came in useful,' he confided to me. 'I took the opportunity of going to look at my first wife's grave, and when I got back to the car I found it still in the same place.'

I never met his first wife but I met Ethel, his second, and liked her very much. They had two children, Punch and Juliette.

Ethel took rooms for him in a house near Windsor when he came over from America to do *Rolls-Hyphen-Royce*. At lunch one day I asked him where he was staying and he told me, adding, 'Before I came over I kept wondering why Ethel had rooms in that house, but when I got here I soon found out!' Sure enough, next year Ethel married the proprietor.

Wilfrid was fond of racing when he lived in England, and still more of betting.

One story I heard straight from the horse's mouth is that of his first encounter with a bookmaker. Wilfrid's father was a canon of the Church of England, and lived down in Gloucestershire. One afternoon, according to his son, the young Wilfrid was playing with his bricks in his father's study. The bell rang downstairs, and his father said, 'Go down and tell him I'm not in, my boy.'

Obediently Wilfrid went down, opened the front door and saw a large man in a check suit standing there. 'And that, my boy, was the first bookie I ever saw,' he told me.

To return to Tony Quayle, I got to know him better when he did *After the Ball Is Over* with his Compass Company, which he formed some years before his death. He played the Duke of Drayton MFH, and Patrick Cargill played his butler. We opened in Bath, toured for a few months, then went to the Old Vic but progressed no further.

The critics were fiercely divided in their views. Which school was correct in their assessment, who can tell. We will get an answer, no doubt, when the play becomes due for revival in due course. Meanwhile, one thing is certain — producing it was a noble undertaking on the part of Tony Quayle.

Since then I have had only one play on in the West End. Called *Portraits*, first produced at the Malvern Festival and then, after a provincial tour, at the Savoy Theatre in London in 1987, it dealt with the subject of Augustus John. I had read the life of him by Michael Holroyd, which I much enjoyed, and instantly made up my mind to write a play about him. I had always found him interesting, and liked the portrait of my mother-in-law which he did of her when she was young, though he made her look much older than she does now at the age of ninety!

I still laugh too at my father-in-law's remark when I told him that when I had gone to pick his daughter up from the studio of an artist called Anthony Devas who was doing a portrait of her, in order to take her out to lunch, I had found the door locked. 'That's all right,' he said, 'don't worry. He does that to keep Augustus John out.'

As a result, I wrote the play in a good mood and with particular interest. It was put on at the Malvern Festival in May 1987. Its director was John Dexter, who, with Lindsay Anderson, had been a star director at the Royal Court Theatre under George Devine.

Keith Michell played the part of Augustus John, while the parts of General Montgomery, Matthew Smith and Cecil Beaton were all taken by Simon Ward. Pamela Lane played Dorelia and Michael Wordsworth, Bernard Shaw.

I could not fault them when I saw them at the dress-rehearsal, and, as I expected, the play went well in Malvern.

After a long tour we reached the Savoy. For some reason, which is hidden from me still, the theatre was three parts empty on the first night.

I had never experienced such a thing before, and I trust I will never do so again, since all those feelings of excitement and anticipation that are customary on a first night with a full house disappeared completely. Normally on first nights the auditorium is filled with nurses and taxi-drivers, as well as with friends of those connected with the play.

Why, on this sad occasion, this routine was not observed I do not know. The cast performed extremely well, but Rachel and I and those friends and relatives who had come with us in anticipation of a happy evening left the theatre in deep depression, unrelieved by dinner in a private room at the Savoy at which, for the first time in my life, anticipating no financial return from the play in the near future, I required my guests — apart from family and those connected with the play — to pay for their meal.

The reviews were not unfriendly, but the play never got off the ground. Its closure could have been marred by tragedy. One night during the last week, Simon Ward was found by his wife, passed out in the hall of their house. He had evidently been assaulted on his way home, and had just made it to his house after crawling along the pavement. Despite this, he went on stage again the next night, which was a Friday, and for both performances on Saturday.

That Sunday, he went to see a doctor, who arranged for him to be trepanned, as he had damaged his skull badly. He went to recuperate in Italy, in a villa belonging to Zeffirelli, the Italian film director. When I wrote to tell Simon how sad we were to hear of his misfortunes I added a postscript to the effect that the only silver lining to the cloud was that the British public clearly thought the play had come off because of his accident, whereas it had been scheduled to come off in any case.

My last new play to be staged was *The Christmas Truce*, which opened at the Horseshoe Theatre in Basingstoke. It was directed by Ian Mullins, who had earlier directed a new play of mine, as well as some revivals, at the Redgrave Theatre in Farnham when he was in charge there. The set of the no-man's-land between the British and the German lines in 1914 was designed by Vikie le Saché, and was about the best of its kind that I have ever seen.

I hope this play will be revived one day, in which case I would like to have the same director, the same set designer and the same outstanding cast of actors, both British and German, as in Basingstoke.

George Waring, who played Colonel Reid, is another hero of mine: he is the kind of actor that I keep my eye on, since he is coming up to the age at which many of my leading parts would suit him.

I first met him in Salisbury some twenty years ago, when he played the lead in my play *Betzi* about Napoleon on St Helena, which told of how the defeated Emperor fell in love with Betzi Balcombe, the daughter of an East India Company manager.

Among actors of whom I am fond, I must say something of Robert Morley. I have yet to see him in a play of mine, although I once wrote one for him and Uncle Wilfrid, called *A Friend In Need*. Had they done it, as both I and Robin Fox, then Robert's agent, strongly recommended, there is not much doubt that it would have been a big hit. But they were worried, as I see it, about which was the best part and turned it down in case the day should dawn when one of them would learn that the best part was not his.

Some years later Robert booked himself to do *After The Ball Is Over* — the play which Tony Quayle eventually put on with Compass — but this also fell through, though for a very different reason. He trod on a jellyfish while out in Australia, where one of his sons lives, and this caused him to give up the idea of performing in the play. Indeed, he has not trodden the boards since for reasons best known to himself. The story goes, however, that the jellyfish has been back at work for some time!

Of the film actors I have liked, the ones I knew best were James Mason and David Niven.

Just before the War I appeared with James in a play by Dodie Smith. He gave a good performance, though it was hard to hear what he was saying — as Murray MacDonald, the director, never ceased telling him. Indeed, he went so far as to advise a career on the films, instead of on the stage!

I also met David Niven just before the War, when he was married to his first wife who, most tragically, fell down a lift-shaft while playing some after-dinner game. He spent the War with the Astor brothers in the Phantom Reconnaissance Regiment. The next time we met was in Los Angeles, where he had a nice house. The next-door house was owned by a rich man — Bill Durney, the head of Carnation Milk, whose wife wrote *Seven Brides For Seven Brothers*. Bill once told me that the telephone rang on the evening that he and his wife moved into their new house. When he picked it up and said 'Hello', a voice said, 'My name's David Niven. Are you all right?'

'Yes, I think so,' Bill replied. 'Why do you ask?'

'Well,' David answered, 'there are lots of vultures circling above your house, so I thought I'd better make sure.' Then he rang off.

In the television world amongst my favourites with whom I have worked on my television plays — apart from Wendy Hiller, Cyril Cusack and Rex Harrison — I number Denholm Elliott and Michael Hordern. These two acted on the small screen in a play of mine called *You're All right, How Am*

I?, which is about a patient being interviewed by a psychiatrist.

I went to its first reading at the BBC and, as we sat down, the director said, 'Let's read it through first, shall we?'

Michael started off with the first line, at which Denham raised his head and asked if the director would come outside with him for a moment.

Out they went, returning a few minutes later. 'OK, Michael, carry on,' said the director. Michael did so.

In the lunch break, I asked the director what had been worrying Denholm at the start.

'Oh,' said he, with a smile, 'he just thought he was playing Michael's part and Michael his, that's all.'

Regardless of this minor hitch, Denholm performed to perfection the part he had failed to study, and vice versa.

Since I no longer get my plays into the West End, I enjoy visiting those local theatres which stage revivals of my erstwhile hits. The play they do most is one of my favourites, *Lloyd George Knew My Father*.

Recently we went to Southwold, where the summer theatre is run by Jill Freud, Clement Freud's wife. Apart from running the theatre, she puts up all the actors, feeds them when they get home late at night and takes the female lead in many of the plays as well. She gave an excellent performance in the part of Lady Boothroyd of the byepass.

Jill, whom I first met when she was in *The Dame of Sark*, in the West End, playing the maid Cecile to Celia's dame, is extremely good on stage, apart from being indefatigable. I have seen quite a few productions of *Lloyd George Knew My Father* since it was on in London, but never one so superbly done as that.

The set was as good as one could hope for in a theatre of that size. The director was Nat Brenner. Under his skilled hand, timing, atmosphere and interpretation were all faultless. Not for years have I left a theatre in which a play of mine was being performed feeling quite so happy.

Not long afterwards we went to see the same play in The Mill, in Sonning. I had no idea that it was on until I read a favourable notice in the *Maidenhead Advertiser*, which began 'It was rather flattering to find the *Advertiser* featured on stage in *Lloyd George Knew My Father*. Lady Boothroyd is incensed when she picks up her local paper — apparently a recent edition of the *Advertiser* — and finds that the byepass against which she has campaigned is going ahead.'

When one reads the press these days about the M3 and the M this and the M that, one can be forgiven, I hope, for remarking of a play first written twenty years ago, 'How topical can one get?' I find the omens good for a revival in the West End at the hands of some enlightened impresario!

Before closing this chapter I would like to say that, in a long life, I have yet to meet an actor or an actress with whom I have not got on extremely well - except perhaps for Uncle Wilfrid on that one occasion when he buggered up *Rolls-Hyphen-Royce* before the stage lights had been on for more than half a minute. But I did not quarrel with him even then — indeed as far as I remember we gave him supper!

What I like about all actors — again barring Uncle Wilfrid on that one occasion — is their loyalty. Whatever they may say behind one's back — and they may say a lot for all I know — when it comes to a meeting they invariably look me in the eye and give me their support. If this is merely acting, then I am, of course, a sucker, but I like to think that it is not. I also like to think it is sincerity and, in this case, not based on insincerity!

CHAPTER 11

T heatrical directors come in different shapes and sizes. Some are modest and hard-working, others are flamboyant and erratic; both groups may, on occasions, be brilliant as well.

Nowadays a new group is emerging. They are still in a minority, but there are disturbing signs that their numbers are increasing.

I am always writing letters to *The Times* (and sometimes they get printed) about what I read in their dramatic critics' notices to the effect that one of Shakespeare's plays has been 'adjusted' at the whim of the director. Sometimes I am profoundly irritated by the actors' costumes — such as, for example, when I read that an actor on his way to be beheaded was dressed in white tie and tails.

Another production put on at Stratford portrayed one of Shakespeare's kings who had just taken over from his conquered predecessor, talking to his subjects on the television, much as the Queen does in her Christmas broadcast each year.

After reading about one or other of these outrages — or both — I wrote to Bernard Levin, asking him to write an article in *The Times* condemning such atrocities. He wrote back to say I was lucky not to be addicted to the opera, as he was, because he had recently attended a production of some eighteenth-century work during the last act of which a troop of motorcyclists had appeared on stage!

Shortly before I started on this chapter I discovered, to my horror, that it is not only theatre and opera directors who commit such sacrilege. A *Times* review by Benedict Nightingale informed the world that Alan Ayckbourn, no less, had seen fit to join the infidels.

'Othello is Othello is Othello,' Nightingale wrote in disgust, I was glad to note — 'a living organism in spite and, perhaps, because of its imperfections. What would Ayckbourn think of a literary pro who tidied up the Divine Comedy or Revelations?' After reading that, I wrote another letter to *The*

Times to ask how Ayckbourn would feel if I readjusted one of his plays and then put it on in some provincial theatre. The answer, I predicted, was that he would almost certainly sue me since he holds the copyright in all his plays, unlike the Bard of Avon who has lost his, having been deceased for more than fifty years. I ended by suggesting that my fellow-playwright should perhaps feel nervous of the trend he has decided to support, when he considers what may happen when that arbitrary date is applied to his own work some time in the future. I have yet to see the letter printed.

On a wider issue, I consider that the law of copyright is grossly unfair anyway. Why should the rights in all my plays go public fifty years after my death when, to make only one comparison, Sir Alec's heirs could retain his house and estates for centuries to come — always assuming that they can afford to do so.

To return to my theme — those directors with whom I have worked — Colin Chandler master-minded my first two successes after the War. I first met him when *Now Barabbas* came on at the Boltons Theatre. He directed it both there and later in the West End, after Tom Arnold and O'Brien, Linnit and Dunfee had transferred it to London. When *The Chiltern Hundreds* followed it there, Colin was engaged by the same management to direct that as well. Nor was he awed in any way by the formidable A.E. Matthews, who was more than twice his age. Indeed the young director and the aged star shared their great triumph jointly and deservedly when the play opened in the West End.

The last play Colin directed for me was *The Thistle and The Rose*, which was about King James IV of Scotland's death on Flodden Field, where 'shivered was fair Scotland's spear and broken was her shield', according to Sir Walter Scott. To judge from what I read about the period in my research, Sir Walter was in no way guilty of exaggeration.

Colin read it, liked it and produced it at the Boltons, casting Raymond Westwell, who was in my regiment during the War, as the young king.

As his leading lady — the young English princess who comes up to Scotland to become the king's bride — he selected a young student from the RADA called Dorothy Tutin.

This was her first part as a professional, and she performed it very well.

The play did not transfer to the West End at that time, but a few years later, it had a short session at the Vaudeville. Hugh Burden played the king and Andrew Cruickshank was Lord Angus Bell the Cat — the king's right-hand man, and an ancestor of mine.

I wrote this play originally for the Edinburgh Festival and Colin Chandler — then head of an acting school in Glasgow — recommended it to the committee on which he sat.

But one member of the board rejected it. His name was James Bridie, and he won the day.

On hearing this, I wrote to him, suggesting that it was immoral that one playwright, of whatever eminence, should ban another playwright's work. He wrote back saying that he did not like the play and therefore he had no alternative. I begged to differ. There our correspondence ended.

I still hope that *The Thistle and The Rose* may one day come on during the Festival in the city I was born in, though experience has taught me that I have a tough nut to crack. Another play of mine that I would like to see in Edinburgh is *The Queen's Highland Servant* mentioned earlier.

But prospects are not good, judging by what occurred a few years back when I sent both plays to Frank Dunlop, who ran the Festival at the time. (John Drummond took over from him recently.)

No acknowledgement of their receipt came from the north, so after six or seven months I wrote to Dunlop again, enquiring if the plays had been received and, if so, what was his reaction to them. The same silence ensued.

When a year or more was up, I wrote a private letter to the *Scotsman*, asking if the editor could help me find out what had happened to them.

He wrote back sympathetically, assuring me that he would make discreet enquiries for me. Some weeks later both plays were returned — unread, I imagine.

Nor was Frank Dunlop the only Scottish impresario to disappoint me.

When one of my agents, Eric Glass, sent copies of both

plays to six or seven other theatres and managements in Scotland, only a minority replied to the effect that they were booked up for that season and the next, but that if there was ever a vacancy they would think about them. The remainder, I imagine, still have copies somewhere in their offices.

I may sound bitter when I write about this episode but, if I do, I like to think that I may be excused, if only on the grounds that a wee Scots lad like myself deserves a wee bit better treatment at the hands of his compatriots. 'Oh Scotia, my dear my native land.'

That line penned by Sir Walter Scott and five or six of the ensuing lines can be read on a stone on Coldstream Bridge mid-way across the Tweed.

I mention that because it gives me an excuse to tell of something that occurred at the beginning of the War — an episode which brings a smile to my face every time I think of it. It seems that Coldstream Council had the slab removed because they feared the verse inscribed thereon might be of help to any German parachutist who happened to land on the bridge!

To get back to the theatre, the sequel to *The Chiltern Hundreds*, *The Manor of Northstead*, was directed by Wallace Douglas, who died recently. It was not long before we became good friends.

Wally had been a prisoner in Colditz after being captured in France in May 1940. Having written the script of *The Colditz Story* film not long before we met, I naturally found it fascinating to discuss his time there. Indeed I often found myself wishing I had met him earlier.

My favourite story of the many that he told me concerned the occasion when he was performing in a prison play in the role of a German general.

At curtain fall, he had a brilliant idea. On his way back to his quarters with the other actors, he decided that the uniform that he was wearing, borrowed no doubt from the Commandant, might come in very useful were he to continue wearing it instead of handing it in.

On the instant, therefore, he about-turned, walked into the courtyard of the Castle and, from there, towards the guardroom at the main gate.

As he neared it, he heard shouted orders, followed by a turn-out of the guard, the officer-in-charge no doubt mistaking him for a guest of the Commandant, invited in to watch the play.

The officer saluted Wally, who inspected the guard, and then walked out of the open gates to what might have been freedom.

In the darkness he then proceeded on foot to the nearest railway station, took a first-class ticket to Berlin and boarded the next train.

This was his downfall. Some train official came along and asked for his identity card, just as he was settling down for a good night's sleep. The next day he was returned to Colditz to resume his blossoming theatrical career, which prospered once the War was over.

Wally liked *The Manor of Northstead*, which was more than A.E. Matthews did. In fact, Matty steadfastly refused to do it on the grounds that a successful sequel to *The Chiltern Hundreds* was only a pipe-dream.

Shortly after this setback, I met a lady journalist in Glasgow to whom I recounted the sad tale. She printed an account of it that afternoon.

A few days later, I received a letter from a schoolmaster in Castle Douglas in Kirkcudbrightshire informing me that he and his wife — both enthusiastic amateurs — would like to read the play. I sent it to him by return of post and got a letter from him, some days later, saying that the play would be performed on 27 March and on 28 March of the following year and that, if I would like to see it, he would strongly recommend a visit on the 28th when it would be in better shape than on the previous night.

When the time came, Rachel and I went to Castle Douglas with Wally in tow and passed a very pleasant evening at the play.

On our return to London, Wally travelled down to Bushey Heath to call on Matty and assured him that the play came over very well on stage and that, with him in the lead, it would come over that much better.

After prolonged discussion and a few drinks, Matty

was persuaded. It ran for a year.

Another play that Wally did for me was *Aunt Edwina*, starring Henry Kendall. Henry played a retired Guards colonel, a Master of Hounds, who had mistakenly taken a concoction that the vet had prescribed for his horse. As a result he turned into a woman.

I have written at great length about this play in the past and will not repeat the story here. Suffice to say that, in my view, if ever any play of mine deserves a revival, that one does. Indeed, it gets them sometimes in the provinces, but it has yet to get one in the West End.

The Reluctant Debutante's director, Jack Minster, I have discussed already, and there is not much that I can add to that. My happiest memory of him — apart from that production — was a holiday he spent with us in Italy when I was writing a film script. He wore a pair of yellow trousers on the beach at Anzio, where we were staying. I had never seen him dressed with such abandon or so ready for a laugh. What made him laugh the most was when I told him what our nannie had said to the Longman nannie - Mark Longman, Liz his wife and their children were all staying with us — when I drove the two nannies into Rome one morning.

I had assumed that their first view of the Coliseum would fill them with awe. And sure enough, as it came into view, the pair of them in the back seat kept silent. Then the voice of our nannie rang out, and it said this, 'Well, I never, Nannie Longman, they have trolleybuses here, I see — like we do.'

Robin Midgeley, who directed *Lloyd George Knew My Father* in the West End, is a very good director, and I greatly enjoyed my sessions going through the script with him before production. I was better placed than he was, having seen it both at Eton and in Boston Lincs where Anthony Roye put it on and directed it himself.

Robin dealt tenderly with Sir Ralph Richardson, who was not at all confident that he had picked a winner. Indeed, it was not until he got to Oxford that the clouds evaporated and he started to enjoy himself.

So happy was I at this welcome change of attitude that I

allowed him to retain a line which he had written in during rehearsals.

It concerned the fate of a mouse that he had found among his diaries in a hat-box at the end of the first scene. During Act II, as I sat in my seat at Oxford watching the play, I saw Ralph cross over to the bird-cage on the wall during a pause and say to Peggy Ashcroft, 'Mousie's getting on well with the budgerigar.'

In memory of Ralph that line is in the printed version of the play, published by Samuel French.

Murray MacDonald, the director of *The Jockey Club Stakes*, was a friend of mine from before the War: he had directed the Dodie Smith play, *Bonnet Over the Windmill*, which had provided me with my first acting part in the West End.

Twenty years later I saw no change in him. He was as debonair and charming as ever, and very tactful with the leading actor, Alastair Sim, who was full of good ideas about both the script and the production.

Geoffrey Sumner and Bob Coote — the Colonel Pickering of *My Fair Lady* — were Sim's co-stewards. All went merry as a marriage bell, even after Wilfrid Hyde White had replaced Alastair after his contract ended.

Only on one occasion did Murray and I jointly put our feet down, and that was when Wilfrid tried to incorporate a piece of his own business into the play by coming on stage with his hat on and then saying, 'Anybody seen my hat?'

After some argument, we swapped that for an under-taking that we would allow him to put in some lines about some racehorses he owned at that time, since we both decided that it was worth anything to keep him happy until his first night.

This strategy paid off at the Duke of York's in London and the following year in New York, where Wilfrid appeared, again with Bob Coote and Geoffrey Sumner.

So good were they that Clive Barnes, the so-called scourge of Broadway, penned a rave review — not something he made a habit of — especially when reviewing *The Secretary Bird* in London!

One of my favourite plays, *The Dame of Sark*, was put on by Ray Cooney as an Oxford Festival production in October 1974, and directed by Charles Hickman. He took untold trouble over it, which much endeared him to me, including a visit to Dame Sybil Hathaway in Sark (a journey that her death before the play came on prevented Rachel, Celia and me from making). Charles also learned everything that I had learned from her autobiography about her wartime ordeal.

The first night was highly satisfactory and good reviews encouraged Ray to take it to the West End, where it settled into Wyndham's for a season.

Lindsay Anderson directed *The Kingfisher*, starring Sir Ralph, Celia and Alan Webb. At one stage, Peter Hall seemed the most likely prospect. Indeed, he and I talked about the play together in his office at the National. I remember that he did not like the ending and thought that it should be changed. I disagreed with him.

Then, due to log-jams at the National at the time, he asked Lindsay to replace him as director, and arranged for the play to be a National production in the West End until the log-jam had broken.

The next thing that happened was that certain West End managers complained that he was using the West End as a convenient substitute for a pre-London tour. Laurence Evans warned me of this quarrel and said that it would harm *The Kingfisher* if it were involved in the dispute. He also notified me that the *Evening Standard* was about to run some articles, which could only fan the flames.

I then decided to ask Peter to release the play, which he did. My next move was to demand from all those West End managers involved in the dispute a promise that they would abandon trying to dictate to any playwright where he ought to place his plays in future. In due course, they gave that promise. One of them, John Gale, put on the play instead of Peter at the National Theatre. Lindsay Anderson directed it.

Lindsay was the first director with a Royal Court background that I had ever worked with. I found the experience completely satisfying. So keen was I to see this legendary figure, with his left-wing reputation, on the racecourse, as it were, that I attended one or two rehearsals. I was not disappointed. He would lie back in his chair in the rehearsal room and watch the cast at work. If he saw something he disapproved of, he would register displeasure by raising his eyebrows as high as they would go, accompanying this with a sardonic smile in my direction.

But he never interrupted — only at the conclusion of the scene did he suggest that certain things might be adjusted with advantage. He was seldom answered back, since all the cast had faith in his judgement — as did the author.

Only once, as I recall, did a quarrel break out, and that was when the lady photographing the production wished to do so at a time which, for some reason, did not suit Sir Ralph. He put his foot down. Lindsay did the same, but in support of the photographer.

I'm not too clear about the outcome, but I rather think that Lindsay had his way for the good reason that it was not easy for Sir Ralph or, for that matter, anybody else, to hold out against his restrained and logical approach to any problem.

Recently, he has read two unacted plays of mine and spoken highly of both.

At the time of writing though, nothing has yet been set up since it is not easy nowadays to flush an impresario from cover and persuade him to embark on a production which would have cost around £2,000 to put on thirty years ago, but would now cost £200,000 at a very modest estimate. But more of that in the next chapter, in which I propose to cover impresarios.

Of Lindsay's left-wing reputation — earned, no doubt, at the Royal Court during the heady days of the New Wave — he showed no sign during *The Kingfisher*, remaining totally impartial from start to finish. Only recently did I encounter a trace of it when he told me that the ending of my play about the Thatchers (never performed) ought to be much stronger.

'In what way?' I asked him.

'Well,' he said, 'you end it with the new PM providing them both with peerages.'

'That's right,' I said. 'What's wrong with that?'

'I've already told you,' Lindsay said. 'It ought to be much stronger.'

'And I have already asked you in what way,' I told him.

'Well, what's wrong with Denis shooting her?' said Lindsay.

'Everything,' I said, 'as you know damned well.'

There the conversation ended, not to be renewed.

I once asked Sir Ralph why he thought that Lindsay had assumed his left-wing mantle. 'Well, apart from the Royal Court,' he told me, 'I think he's got a chip on his shoulder.'

'Oh, why's that?' I asked.

'Because', said Ralph, 'his father was a general in the Indian Army.'

Which reminds me that I have a photograph of Lindsay Baby (as Celia called him) sitting in a solar topee on the barrel of a cannon, with a Sepoy sentry standing on guard over his small figure. When he reads this, he will take no action save to raise his eyebrows and then switch on his sardonic smile.

John Dexter, Lindsay's colleague at the Royal Court, also with a left-wing reputation, equally unfounded, was less of an introvert than Lindsay. In fact, he was merry as a grig (whatever that may be) except when somebody enraged him when the feathers — though not often his — would fly.

When he directed *Portraits*, which I mentioned earlier when writing about Simon Ward, he did so beautifully. His sincerity was such that actors automatically responded to it; while his charm was such that he could swing even the ultra-obstinate with honeyed phrases and a twinkle in his eye towards his point of view. His great friend Riggs O'Hara, always ready to dispel the storm clouds with a quip, was devastated by John's death. I wish him well wherever he may be today.

The fact that I — an ultra-right-wing playwright in the minds of many drama critics due to my aristocratic background — should get on so famously with two Royal Court directors gives me acute pleasure, since it reinforces my profound conviction that all those who seek to place the theatre in a political arena are not only wrong, but wilfully misguided.

There is no political division in the theatre save that which is imposed on it by certain writers in the press who automatically assume that, since they wish it to be so, it must be.

On the contrary, it should be — and would be, were it not for all the propaganda put out by some sections of the media — a wholly non-political profession.

This does not mean that political plays, written as such, should not see the light of day — only that the criticism they attract should be based solely on artistic content. This is a subject that I mean to deal with in the next chapter, when I write about the hangover from the New Wave and its near substitution by the Theatre of Subsidy, which tends to be divisive *vis-à-vis* the West End.

A director I am much addicted to is Ian Mullins. I first got to know him when he ran the Redgrave Theatre in Farnham. He directed one new play of mine, *David and Jonathan*, there and several revivals, and he was extremely bold to put on *A Christmas Truce* in the beginning of 1989, since it has a cast of fifteen, all male.

The first production of R.C. Sheriff's classic, *Journey's End*, was bedevilled at the start of its career for the same reason.

West End managers who read it told its author that they would only consider putting it on if he would write in some female roles. Quite rightly, he refused to do so, pointing out that dug-outs on the Western Front did not have any women in them nor was he inclined to write them in, thus falsifying history.

As a result, years went by before he got it put on, and then only after he had gone up to Birmingham and given it to an adventurous director called Maurice Browne, over supper in the Midland Hotel. Sheriff pretended that he happened to be passing through Birmingham, whereas in fact he had hurried up there after someone told him Maurice Browne liked taking risks.

The same applies to Ian Mullins — which is why I gave *A Christmas Truce* to him, because I knew that he would stand at my right hand and fight off any suggestions about including women in it. It got a very good reception in Basingstoke from both the audience and the critics. I await the day when it will earn its just reward in the West End.

To return to R.C. Sheriff, I sometimes met him at the Dramatists' Club. At dinner once, Esther MacCracken, the authoress of *Quiet Wedding* and *Quiet Weekend*, both highly successful plays, on whose right hand I was sitting, pushed a menu over to me on which she had written, 'Who is sitting next to me?'

I took my pen out of my pocket and wrote 'William Douglas Home'.

'No, on my other side, you fool,' she wrote back.

'R.C. Sheriff,' I informed her.

I cannot end this chapter without saying something about Anthony Roye, who without doubt was the most adventurous director — not to mention impresario — ever to cross my path.

I met him first when he took on *The Secretary Bird*. He was not the kind of man to have a manager behind him with sufficient money to support him: he was his own manager with little or no money of his own.

And yet he managed somehow. God knows where he got the money from to pay his debts when he produced a flop — or perhaps he never did! At any rate he did not do so with *The Secretary Bird* — far from it.

Tony chose his actors, his scenery and his provincial theatres himself. He usually made his choice of actors from those with whom he had worked in the past, on the principle that a choice once made should be persevered with. And, of course, he used to play the lead himself. Nor did he think it worthwhile spending money on scenery, when he was able to supply his own. Every stitch of carpet and every stick of furniture on the stage, as well as every yard of curtain, came from his own flat in Wimbledon — which never worried him, since he reckoned that while on tour he would not be at home!

The theatres he chose were those that he had visited before on tour. Evidently he had done well in them, since they were always ready to accommodate him. An exception was the Mowlem Theatre in Swanage, where *The Secretary Bird* opened for its first production on a Monday night, even though the theatre was not officially opened by the mayor until the following Thursday afternoon.

Some of his theatres were quite large, like Plymouth, while others were on the small side — like the one in Street, where Mr Clark makes his shoes (or did when I was in the theatre he built). I also remember visiting a theatre in a private house in the West Country. The last one we played at on that particular tour was in Scunthorpe; there I first met John Gale, who went on to produce the play in the West End precisely one year later.

I profoundly admire Tony Roye, because he did his own thing and he did it his way.

Now he is retired and sadly crippled, but as active in his mind as ever; he is working on a book about a landlady in Manchester and basking, I hope, in at least one playwright's eternal gratitude.

CHAPTER 12

S o far I have written about my favourite actors and directors.
Now it is the turn of managers and critics who, between them,
form the apex of the edifice in which the West End theatre (or the
commercial theatre, as it is known) exists.

The managers whom I will deal with first are those who
have the money-bags or, if they are not affluent themselves,
collect them. Sometimes they are women. One of those I look
back on with gratitude is Anna Deere Wiman, who financed
The Reluctant Debutante. But, almost always, they are men.

The first I ever met was called Anthony Ellis. He put on
my first play, *Great Possessions*, which I wrote at Oxford
and pressed on John Gielgud when he was taking coffee in the
Caledonian Hotel. Anthony was also its director, though the two
jobs are very seldom coupled.

I quarrelled with my manager in his role of director at the
Q because he made me rewrite the last act, and then refused
to scrap the rewrite when I took exception to it at rehearsals —
but I had made it up with him by the time *Great Possessions*
transferred to the Duke of York's for its six-week run there.

I met him once more during the War when he brought an
Ensa party down to Eastwell Park in Kent. He looked a great
deal older; I like to think I saw him looking at my colonel with
fraternal sympathy, no doubt wondering just how long it would
be before I quarrelled with him too.

It was O'Brien, Linnit and Dunfee who took on *Now Barabbas*
at the Boltons and transferred it to the West End.

O'Brien was the husband of Liz Allen; rumour had it
that Bill Linnit was the son of Edgar Wallace (which I don't
believe); while Jack Dunfee, drawn in the Bertie Wooster mould,
was both a Brooklands racing driver and a wag.

O'Brien was a cheerful, optimistic fellow who admired his
lovely wife immensely — as did I and all who came in contact
with her. With Robert Harris, Hubert Gregg and others she
appeared at the Q Theatre in *Passing By* — which might well

have moved to the West End had Hitler not seen fit to move before it into Northern France.

Linnit was the front man of the three and, I would guess, the one who held the casting vote. I always found him quietly friendly, even when watching the firm's money going down the drain, as he did when my play *Ambassador Extraordinary*, about a visitor from Mars, failed to enchant the gallery. When it was produced in London in 1948 Dunfee was more outspoken. I remember that he came up to me back-stage, as the booing from the gallery died down, and drawled, 'The boys at the back of the class were a bit rowdy tonight, weren't they?' This gave me comfort, as did many of the stories I heard about him.

He was a member of the Bentley motor-racing team, and perhaps because his brother Clive had been killed racing at Brooklands, Jack was put in charge of the team when they were in Italy. The team were filling up their cars with English petrol before the race when an Italian official approached Jack and told him that it was against the rules for them to do so, adding that his team would only be allowed to race with native petrol.

Jack held up his hand while he told his frustrated team-mates the dire news, adding that he was going to argue his case in the office. Off he went with the Italian official, while his fellow-drivers started revving up their engines in disgust.

After some time, Jack reappeared, held up his hand again and, in the silence that ensued, said, 'Sorry, boys, we've got to use the school ink after all!'

When I knew him he had a charming wife called Audrey. Later they got divorced, while still remaining on friendly terms. After her remarriage Audrey adopted two small children, much to Jack's amazement.

He was playing croquet once with Kenneth Harper, who worked with him in MCA after O'Brien, Linnit and Dunfee had ceased to function. Some small children were playing somewhat noisily around the fringes of the croquet lawn. Leaning on his mallet, Jack looked across at them and said to Kenneth, 'And to think that Audrey's just bought two of those!'

I lunched with Jack at Claridge's one day and, during the course of the meal, I complained to him about some trauma I was suffering from. I forget its cause, but it could have concerned some new play of mine which his firm had rejected.

He made no reply when I had finished speaking, but instead he took out his note-case and extracted from it a card, which he held up. On it was written, in large capitals, 'YOUR STORY MOVES ME TO TEARS, YOU HAVE ALL MY SYMPATHY.'

He then replaced it in his note-case and continued eating his fried sole.

He and his colleagues put on *The Chiltern Hundreds* immediately after *Now Barabbas*.

Bill Linnit was adamant that nobody but A.E. Matthews ought to be entrusted with the leading role. He warned me that Matty was about to visit the United States, and would have to be approached without delay.

I agreed at once, even though I had never met him at that stage nor seen him in a play. Bill sent the script to Bushey Heath and Matty, bless him, telephoned next day to say that he would take the part.

My relationship was solid with the firm thereafter, notwithstanding the disaster of *Ambassador Extraordinary* in the following year, until the sad day came when Bill died and the firm closed down.

As I said earlier, it was Paul Clift who put on *The Reluctant Debutante*, with Anna Wiman's money. Paul was much the oldest manager I had ever come across — in fact, he was about the same age as I am myself today!

He had an office on top of the Strand Theatre, in which he sat all day, benignly smiling at the stream of visitors who called on him and considering the projects that they laid before him.

I suspect that Paul was always short of money personally — judging by the occasion when I went to see him once about a play that I had written, and he asked if I could lend him some! As far as I remember I wrote out a cheque for a hundred pounds, so creating a precedent in my dealings with impresarios.

Sir Peter Saunders (then plain Peter) came into my life in his capacity as manager of *The Reluctant Peer*. I had not named it that originally because I wanted to continue with the routine I had set up with its two predecessors, both of which involved the same theme and the same family. *The Chiltern Hundreds* and *The Manor of Northstead* are, in fact, the names of two sinecures for which an MP who wishes to give up his seat may apply. I had given my new play the name of a third sinecure, 'The Sequestration of Buckingham', but Peter said that it was too long. Whether I argued that it was shorter than *Witness for the Prosecution*, which he also produced, I cannot now remember.

What I do remember, though, is that he was adamant about long names. He rang me once to say that *Lloyd George Knew My Father* would do better if I changed its name to something shorter, but in this he was mistaken since the play could hardly have done better than it did (and still does) even if it had been called *Ll G*.

Nonetheless, to soothe the feelings of my newest impresario, I called it *The Reluctant Peer* on his suggestion, since the plot concerns a peer who abandons his title before taking over from a sick prime minister — which was, of course, the story of my brother Alec's exit from the House of Lords in order to take on the leadership from Uncle Harold.

The first rehearsal took place on the stage of the Ambassadors, a delightful little theatre in which *The Mousetrap* had been running for some years — and is running still next door to the St Martin's Theatre. My leading lady was the delightful and unpredictable Sybil Thorndike. She opened the East Meon church fête once and started up as follows: 'As a canon's daughter, I can't tell you how delighted I am to be opening your fête on this delightful summer afternoon on behalf of this splendid charity.' Then she paused and called out to the vicar, 'By the way, what is it?'

Talking of *The Moustrap*, I recall a strong rebuke that I received from Peter Saunders — who had come to be associated with *The Mousetrap* — after writing a letter on the subject of the Korean War to the *Spectator*. In it I remarked that one might just as well argue that Sir Winston had not done this or that as argue that the murder in *The Mousetrap* was not done by ---- (and here I gave the name of the murderer, which I shall refrain from doing here).

I received a violent letter from Peter telling me off for 'giving away his secret'. I replied facetiously that what he called his 'secret' was, in fact, disclosed eight times a week to several thousand people.

Nonetheless, I must concede that the majority of those who see the play seem to keep quiet about it.

Apart from putting on *The Jockey Club Stakes* — which in these days of horse-doping should be revived — Peter has turned down many more of my plays than he has produced.

Back in the 1960s, when my *Aunt Edwina* was at the Fortune Theatre, I borrowed £1,500 from Peter to enable me to keep it running for a week or two. He lent me this sum on the understanding that I would submit each new play that I wrote to him, until he had produced three of them. Since I was desperate, I signed this contract, against my agent's advice. Even though I paid him back the sum that I had borrowed almost at once, Peter insisted that the contract should remain in force.

By the late Seventies, he had produced only two out of the many plays that I had written in the intervening years — *The Jockey Club Stakes* and *The Reluctant Peer*. *The Kingfisher* was under option to him, but I begged him not to go ahead, since it was already in the hands of Peter Hall, sent to him at Sir Ralph's request. Peter agreed to release me from this final option, on the understanding that I would submit one more to him to make up for his loss.

Some years later, when Peter asked for yet another option on another play, I called in my solicitor who wrote to Peter asking if the contract could be closed down and on what terms, so that I could place the play elsewhere.

Peter agreed to let me break the contract in exchange for a cheque for a thousand pounds, which I signed in his office in the presence of John Rubinstein, who represents me in the field of law with brilliance and much tolerance.

Peter and I are still friends, and I call him up and tell him Brian Johnston's latest stories once or twice a month. But he has not asked me in recent years to the annual *Mousetrap* lunch at the Savoy — which action (or lack of it rather) may indicate that I am undergoing mild punishment. I am quite prepared to take this with a stiff upper lip, although I much enjoyed the last lunch I went to.

On that occasion Lord Denning made a speech, the opening passage of which is imprinted firmly on my mind. It ran as follows: 'When I was a High Court judge, I dispensed a lot of justice. But when I became an Appeal Court judge, sitting with two others, the odds against dispensing justice dropped to two to one against!'

What more is there to say about Sir Peter Saunders? He loves cricket and sits watching it on television in his office which he retains at the Vaudeville, even though he sold the theatre some years ago. What else he does is hidden from me. All I know for certain is that my bi-monthly telephone calls contain — after 'Johnners' has been dealt with — pleas from me that (in spite of our past differences) he should get up off his arse, switch off the television and produce some new plays of mine even though he no longer has first option on any of them or — if that is too much for him — some revivals. His reply invariably is that he is too old. 'Never mind that, get on with it,' I say over the wires. Then I send my love to Katie Boyle, his wife, and ring off till the next time. Ah well, no luck so far, but I am aware of Bruce's spider, coming as I do from the north end of Coldstream Bridge.

John Gale, a friend of Peter's, who had been responsible for putting on *The Secretary Bird* after Tony Roye's initial tour, also put on *The Kingfisher* after its initial troubles at the National. His casting was impeccable in both plays, as was his choice of director.

For the first, he engaged Philip Dudley, a young man from television with not much experience of theatre but this he quickly acquired. For the second, as you know, he chose Lindsay Anderson.

John is a man of mercurial temper and I must admit to having sometimes quarrelled with him over trivialities, but neither of us ever nurses a grudge. Peter Saunders christened him the yo-yo, thereby neatly illustrating his astonishing capacity for being happy one moment and furious the next.

But never mind how black the clouds are, the storm never lasts long and the sun comes out again with renewed brilliance — until the next forecast of low pressure warns all those who know their John to run for cover once again.

He gave up producing plays in the West End at the start of the Eighties and took on the management at Chichester. Now he has given that up after a successful spell there and has retired nearby to a delightful house with his charming wife Lisel.

We went to lunch with him last summer and I put it to him that he should become an impresario again.

'And do some of your dreadful plays?' he said.

'That's right,' I told him.

'God forbid,' he said and then, since he is nothing if not honest, he went on to say that he had made more money out of me than anybody else during his impresarioship (if that word exists).

I still live in hope that John Gale and 'Mousetrap' Saunders will come together one day to provide their aged friend and benefactor with an opportunity for re-entry into the West End, from which he has been banished for so long.

Ray Cooney produced *Lloyd George Knew My Father* in conjunction with John Gale, after its first amateur production by the boys at Eton College.

When the play came on at the Savoy, I took the boy who had played Sir Ralph's part at Eton to his dressing-room at curtain-fall. I introduced him to Sir Ralph and told him he had played his part at Eton.

'And a great deal better than I did tonight, I would imagine,' said Sir Ralph, as he shook hands.

'Not quite so good, sir,' said the boy, 'but very nearly.'

Ray is an all-rounder — actor, impresario and playwright — and outstandingly efficient in all three departments. He has given up producing plays to concentrate on his acting and playwriting. Recently, the press was full of praise for his new play in the West End.

So much then for the impresarios, or at least some of those with whom I have been involved in the West End. Now for their equivalents in the United States.

The first to put on one of my plays there was Gilbert Miller, who produced *The Reluctant Debutante* in New York. He was a portly character, who had been in the Marines in his youth. I admired him greatly since he had the necessary enthusiasm for whatever project he embarked on.

He saw *The Reluctant Debutante* in London and then came down to lunch, during which he announced that he would put the play on at the Henry Miller Theatre in New York, named after his father.

This he did with Wilfrid Hyde White, who was replaced by Jack Hulbert at the Cambridge. Anna Massey went to New York as well, and her mother, Adrienne Allen, replaced Celia.

Rachel and I attended the first night in New York. To our delight, the play was well-received by the audience that night and by the critics the next morning, which enabled us to go to Hollywood to talk about the film script, via Washington and the Grand Canyon.

A New York producer I have got to know in recent years is Elliott Martin, who put on *The Kingfisher* with Rex Harrison and Claudette Colbert in America. He has shown interest recently in a new play of mine called *Pocket Money*, but has yet to put the chips down.

But the greatest impresario of all, at least on this side of the Atlantic, was Binkie Beaumont, of the firm of H.M. Tennant. One of his distinctions was that he never put on a play of mine, although he got very near to doing so once. Otherwise, he produced a string of cast-iron successes before, during and after the War.

The play of mine he obviously liked a great deal was *The Secretary Bird*. I know this because when he returned the script to me he wrote a most enthusiastic letter, ending with a phrase which has stuck in my mind ever since — 'I dare not do it with the butchers in their present mood.'

The butchers were, of course, those drama critics of that era who were supporting the New Wave, so-called, to the exclusion of all else.

To illustrate the problem that this posed for what one might, by contrast, call an Old Wave playwright like myself, it's relevant to point out that to be a playwright is a hazardous and dangerous profession at the best of times, but doubly so when there are critics who provide no guarantee that even a deserving play will make the grade, since merit is now always the criterion on which certain reviewers base their judgements.

That, no doubt, is why Sir Harold Hobson, doyen of the Critics' Circle, now retired, wrote the following in *The Times Literary Supplement* in July 1984: 'More critical injustice has been done to William Douglas Home than to any other British dramatist of our time.'

Possibly the most persistent critic to indulge in 'Home-baiting' (a phrase much used at Ludgrove when I was a small boy there) was Kenneth Tynan.

Although he was, unarguably, a most penetrating writer, Tynan had two very large political and social chips, one on either shoulder. These are best illustrated by quoting what he said about Sir Terence Rattigan — a passage I came across while researching a piece I wrote about the latter for the *Dictionary of National Biography* — as well as about myself.

Tynan saw fit to call Sir Terry 'the Formosa of the British Theatre' — in other words, he blamed him for engaging in a rearguard action to defend the well-made play. And he sometimes started his reviews of my works with the phrase 'The Honourable William tells us in Act I'. In such ways did he nail his colours to the mast, much as Bernard Levin did at the same time — though nowadays he seems to be regarded as a kind of Socratean sage!

The New Wave critics set out to destroy the 'Old Wave' playwrights, not temporarily, but for ever — which, of course, is wholly against nature, since the theatre can only remain healthy if every type of play, regardless of subject or author, is allowed to leave the starting stalls at level weights with all the other runners, so as to race exclusively on merit.

This means, in effect, that every playwright has the right to choose his themes and his characters — rich or poor — without being penalized. Freedom for the writer, whether of the New Wave or the Old, is essential, since — with the exception of Canute and certain others — we all know that the tide's ebb and flow ensure no permanence for any individual wave. All are in a state of flux. Censoring a particular type of play on political or social grounds is to be discouraged. Of course, all critics are bound to have some kind of bias in their set-ups — they would not be human otherwise — but it would be nice to think that being intelligent men (and sometimes, though not often, women) they would do their best to tone such bias down when they are writing about art.

Yet the evidence proves beyond all doubt that there have been, and maybe still are, critics who quite deliberately indulge their political and social biases in their reviews.

As Harold Hobson once wrote, 'It is a critical convention either to abuse Mr Douglas Home or to condescend to him — this is a tribute that mediocrity often pays to outstanding talent.'

How I love that man!

As for social comment with a big S, a reviewer on the *Daily Mail* wrote of *The Secretary Bird* as follows: 'So long as there are enough upper-class people about with a longing to see other upper-class people portrayed on the stage, it's probably safe to predict that Mr Douglas Home has a popular success on his hands'; while Irving Wardle of *The Times*, commenting on the restoration to favour of WDH, added, in his customary political style, 'It seems that the pendulum is on the move again and no sooner have we had a quick gulp of fresh air than we go scurrying back to the burrow.'

Take Irving Wardle's review of my play *The Dame of Sark*, produced in London in 1974.

> WDH takes the story of the wartime occupation of Sark so as to combine two escapist fantasies. For Sark itself, where the crumbling class connections still flourished. Then there is the war, which, by his account came over as a well-bred affair waged according to the old code of honour.
>
> Colonel Count von Schmettau was portrayed as a gallant soldier of the old school, loyally carrying out the orders of a government of which he is ashamed. That of course raises the question of German obedience.

Then came the punch line: 'But Mr Home is not one to open that can of beans.'

Wild as that accusation makes me every time I read it, having spent a year in prison at the end of the War for opening that very can of beans — the question of obedience — I will leave it to Harold Hobson to refute that charge on my behalf.

Reviewing *The Dame of Sark* in the *Sunday Times*, he wrote,

'The striking merit of the play is that almost unconsciously the growing realization breaks in upon us that the person who is really almost frighteningly threatened is not the Dame at all but Colonel von Schmettau.'

Another example of the 'social line' in drama criticism was provided by Michael Billington, writing in the *Guardian* about *Betzi*, my play about Napoleon's last years on St Helena: 'At least the play shows a retrospective compassion for the marooned hero and suggests that, though brought up in it, Mr D.H. has great contempt for the English Public School code.' Presumably this was a laboured reference to Sir Hudson Lowe, the British Governor. On an earlier occasion Irving Wardle had weighed in, in 1977, with a review of *In The Red*, my play about a dramatist and his bank manager: 'Here again, WDH gallops forth in defence of an English elite imperilled by the bureaucratic dragon. In *Lloyd George Knew My Father* he championed the propertied classes. This time it is the over-taxed artist.'

The *Financial Times'* critic endorsed this view: 'As usual it is likely to strike a chord with an aristocratic well-heeled audience, disposed to laugh at the problems of an upper-middle class household feeling the pinch.'

And the *Guardian*, of course, took a similar line. Their critic, Nicholas de Jongh, wrote, 'You can imagine WDH scheming up this little atrocity. "How about a playwright," he thinks, "a pleasant upper-middle class fellow like myself — though nothing aristocratic — what?"'

Those quotes should serve to show that not only are some drama critics prejudiced politically and socially against playwrights like myself, but that this non-artistic approach has been noticed by their more enlightened colleagues — and by at least one of those who employed them.

David Astor, a school friend and the former proprietor and editor of the *Observer*, wrote to me a few years ago expressing his astonishment, in retrospect, at how consistently unpleasant Kenneth Tynan had been to me over the years, which proves how democratic the relationship between an editor and his employee must be — at least in the *Observer* — since Ken Tynan was allowed to go on persecuting his employer's friend without rebuke.

At the present time, prospects of getting new plays on are worse than they have ever been, since costs have risen in the theatre beyond all reason, with the result that there are not many impresarios around prepared to take a risk.

Indeed, so desperate did I become to get my play about the Thatchers, *Retirement Age*, put on before it was too late that I inserted an anonymous advertisement in *The Times*, asking for a manager, subsidized or commercial, professional or amateur, prepared to put on a two-handed political comedy. But answer came there none!

CHAPTER 13

I have been lucky in my friends over the years, and many of them have been mentioned already in these pages.

This does not mean that I have special favourites: I delight in all of them, regardless of their origins or the impact they may — or may not — have made on life.

The fact that I have written more about some than about others does not mean that I find their company more pleasing or their intellect more stimulating, only that the things I remember about them are more likely to amuse my readers, particularly if they have heard of them already as public figures.

That is why, encouraged by my publisher, I mean to devote this chapter exclusively to Brian Alexander Johnston, licensed buffoon, freelance BBC man, distributor of doubtful postcards to his friends in hospital, relentless raconteur, life member of Lords, after-dinner speaker and ex-Grenadier — to list only a few of his achievements.

Added to this, I have known him ever since he was a cheeky schoolboy, fitted out with a long nose, which earned him the nickname of 'Hookey' at a very early age.

I got to know him early in my Eton career. He was very friendly, always laughing, always helpful, totally unpatronizing and a good companion, much admired by boys and masters alike.

I recall one episode from his career in Mr Huson's house — my own housemaster was a Mr Howson — although Brian did not tell me about it at the time. No doubt, he thought, perhaps correctly, that it would mature with age.

It seems that there was a boy in Huson's house who wrote home from school to his father to say how, when he was a Lower Boy, a year or two earlier, an older boy, no longer in the school, had made a pass at him; and that this had put him off his work, resulting in a poor examination mark that term (or half, to use the Eton jargon).

He evidently told his father this to counteract some criticism he had made of him during the holidays for not gaining a higher place when he transferred to the Upper School.

The father got in touch with Dr Alington at once, and he in turn told Mr Huson of the episode. He called his house together after prayers one evening and enquired if any of them had had trouble of that nature when the now departed boy had been a member of the house.

To his amazement, though his house was full of pretty little boys with eye-lashes a foot long, any one of whom he thought might well have been a victim of the predator in question, only one boy in the whole house raised his hand in answer to his question. 'I did, sir,' said Hookey.

At this, or so the story goes, Mr Huson, looking dazed as though he had been struck between the eyes by something very heavy, pulled himself together partially, and said, 'All right, you can all go now, boys, except for Johnston.'

As they filed out, Mr Huson went towards his drinks tray and poured himself a treble whisky. As soon as the room was empty he turned to Brian and asked, 'Well, what happened, Johnston?'

'He came to my room one night, sir,' Brian said, 'to tell me that I would be playing cricket for the junior house side the next day.'

'Go on, Johnston,' Mr Huson said.

'And then he put his hand under the sheet, sir,' Brian said.

'And what did you do?' Mr Huson asked, disguising his surprise as best he could.

'I told him to remove it forthwith,' Brian answered.

'Well done, Johnston,' Mr Huson said. 'Goodnight.'

As Brian left the room, his story goes (and who shall doubt it?), he saw his housemaster moving towards the drinks tray, empty glass in hand, to pour himself a second treble.

There are those, of course, who say one shouldn't believe a word that Brian says, but I do not subscribe to that view. Every story he has ever told me (apart from those imported from elsewhere in Christmas crackers or via the City) invariably has a grain of truth in it, however polished up it may have been in the telling.

He ended up in Pop at Eton (as did I, although I had

no colours) as he was a member of the Twenty-Two — the second cricket eleven — and was much loved by all the players on both sides in all the matches that he played in.

When he got to Oxford, which he loved, he continued with his cricket, though he never reached the heights. Perhaps he talked too much behind the wicket, with the result that he got out a good many batsmen, not by catching or stumping them, but rather by diminishing their concentration.

On one occasion he came up before the Dean of New College after having had a motor accident while travelling at seventy mph.

'What speed were you going, Johnston?' asked Dean Henderson.

'Oh, about thirty, sir,' said Brian.

The Dean sighed and said, 'No wonder you have accidents when going at that break-neck speed.'

Before the War we shared a house together in South Eaton place, while I was on the stage and he was working in the City.

I remember visiting the Bag of Nails one night with Michael Astor. Milly Hoey, who ran it, was always friendly with her clientele and made sure that young ladies were available for dancing and, for those who fancied further entertainment, a lot more. Incidentally, Milly's clients seldom signed the visitors' book with their own names, using instead such names as Cyril Alington or Lionel Ford, the Headmaster of Harrow.

Michael asked me where Brian was that evening.

'In bed,' I remember answering, 'because he's had a long day at the Test Match.'

'Playing in it?' Michael asked, facetiously.

'No, watching it,' I told him.

Michael's face assumed a mischievous expression and he turned to the companion Milly had provided for him.

'We've both got a friend,' he told her, 'who is very shy and wouldn't ever dream of coming here. So will you come back to the house he shares with William in South Eaton Place and, if he isn't interested, we'll pay up?'

'Certainly,' she said.

So off we went in Michael's car, arrived at 35 South Eaton Place and went into the sitting-room.

Then, after a short drink, we quietly opened Brian's bedroom door, listened for a moment to the sound of rhythmic breathing, interspersed with the occasional snore, showed in the young lady, shut the door again and went back to the sitting-room.

We had another drink or two and then opened Brian's door again, as quietly as we could — only to hear him giving the young lady from the Bag of Nails a ball-by-ball account of that day's Test Match at the Oval.

Unable to control our merriment, we switched on the light and, to our delight, saw Brian sitting up in bed describing an innings by Hobbs or Sutcliffe to a fascinated audience of one, perched at its far end. We apologized for breaking up the party, and told the girl that we would take her back from whence she came.

She got up, and Brian shook her hand and thanked her for her company. As we shut the door, we heard (or so I like to think) the rhythmic breathing and the intermittent snoring start up again.

With the outbreak of war, Brian joined the Grenadiers while I went into the Fire Service. 'Once a Grenadier,' he used to tell me then, just as he tells me still, 'always a Grenadier.'

He made a great success of it, what's more — which shows that Guardsmen are a lot more tolerant than many people think. By this, I do not mean that he did not conform to discipline. He did, but in what I can best describe as an eccentric way. In other words, his sense of humour or, as some might say, his buffoonery took precedence.

For example, a staff officer was instructing a class of Sandhurst cadets on the duties of an infantry officer.

'In that little copse on the hill over there', he told them, 'is a company of German infantry supported by a troop of tanks. You and your company are down here on the low ground. What steps would you take to overcome them?' He pointed at a certain long-nosed member of his audience and barked out, 'Johnston.'

'Very long ones in the opposite direction, sir,' said Brian. There was a short hush, then laughter broke out, in which the staff officer joined heartily. Nor did he report Cadet Johnston to the Commandant, because no doubt he understood instinctively that Brian was a loyal fellow, who could be relied on in all circumstances.

Later in the War I met another officer who exercised similar restraint. I was proceeding in my baby Fiat to Devonshire, where I was stationed.

On the way down, I stopped off in Bournemouth, where a regiment of Grenadiers was stationed, having been invited by Lieutenant Johnston to partake of luncheon in the mess. The meal concluded, we moved to the sitting-room where Lieutenant Johnston offered his commanding officer a chair.

'Thanks, Brian,' said the unsuspecting colonel — and then as he sat down, Brian pulled the chair away. I looked down at the floor but, much to my surprise, I saw the colonel laughing with the rest of us.

We met again at Bovington when Brian's regiment and mine were being turned over to tanks. On one memorable morning, I came across Brian, Willie Whitelaw and another Grenadier who became a judge in later years but whose name escapes me. Their faces were wreathed in smiles, so I asked them what was going on. They told me their instructor had just gone off to the Naafi after taking every nut and bolt out of the engine of their tank.

'What for?' I asked.

'To make us put them back,' said Brian.

Evidently the instructor had put all the nuts and bolts on a tarpaulin and then given orders that they were to be in place again when he returned.

Intrigued, I lit a cigarette and waited for the instructor to return. After a few minutes he did so, looking much refreshed.

'All right, gentlemen,' he said. 'You finished?'

All three nodded.

'Good,' said the instructor. 'If everything's in order, you can go off to the Naafi yourselves in a brace of shakes.'

At that he disappeared into the engine, only to surface again in a few moments, frowning.

'They're not in position, not the half of them,' he said.

'No?' all three of his students cried, their eyebrows raised.

'No's right,' said the instructor. 'Turn your pockets out and let's see where them missing nuts and bolts is.'

Brian promptly turned out his pockets and then Willie turned out his. No trace of nuts and bolts in any of them.

Finally the future judge turned out his pockets with a confident smile — which soon left his face as nuts and bolts cascaded from them in profusion, much to his surprise.

'All right,' said the instructor, turning to Brian and Willie. 'You two gentlemen can go off to the Naafi while you, sir' — and the contempt he put into that last word still lingers in my mind to this day — 'will stay here until I'm satisfied that every man-jack of them nuts and bolts is back in place where they belong.'

Off sloped Brian and Willie, followed by myself. When we reached the Naafi, they told me through their laughter that, when they found themselves quite unable to replace the nuts and bolts correctly, they had stealthily inserted them into the pockets of their colleague's denims.

Nor were they found out, because the future judge, being a gentleman, never considered splitting on them for one moment. No doubt in later life he hoped that, one day, one or both of them would come up before him, thus allowing him a golden opportunity to get his own back.

Once the course at Bovington was over, Brian's and my paths did not cross again until the War had ended. Indeed, Brian told me once that he felt bad about not writing to me when I was incarcerated, even though he strongly disapproved of me, believing as he did (and still does) that an order is an order and must be carried out, regardless of its content.

When I came out, I learned that he had got the Military Cross, and I asked how he got it.

'Don't be so inquisitive,' he said.

'But I would like to know,' I told him. 'After all, you are my friend — or aren't you?'

'Well, what do you want to know?' he asked.

'What your citation said,' I told him.

'All right, I'll tell you if you really want to know, you nosey bugger,' he said.

Then the story came out. 'It began', he said, 'like this: "This officer, with incredible courage, went at the enemy with cold steel."'

'But how could you have done so?' I interrupted. 'You were a Technical Adjutant in a tank regiment and you wouldn't have had any cold steel with you, except perhaps for a spanner!'

'That's right,' Brian said.

'Then why did your colonel write such a thing?' I asked.

'He didn't,' Brian said.

'Who did, then?' I enquired.

'Me,' Brian answered.

'What!' I said, dumbfounded.

'I was sitting in his tent one afternoon and he was writing out citations,' Brian explained. 'He threw one over to me and said, "I'm getting tired of doing these, so you can do your own." And so I did.'

So there the matter rests — and there, on Brian's chest at regimental dinners and the like, the medal rests as well. Never mind who composed the citation, one can be quite sure that it was well earned.

Out in Germany, just after the War had ended, Brian became his unit's entertainment officer, arranging concerts for the troops and sometimes doing turns himself. Whether through Brian himself or some other agency, this reached the ears of Seymour de Lobinaire, a BBC executive. Aware of his potential, Seymour sent him into Piccadilly Circus one fine summer evening with a microphone with instructions to waylay passersby and ask them about their families, their loves and hates, their children, and whatever else came into his mind.

The response was more than adequate, convincing Seymour that he had discovered a potential interviewer with a cheerful disposition and marked talent.

From that evening on, Brian never looked back. He became a leading figure in a weekly programme called 'In Town Tonight' and some of his unlikely contributions remain firmly in my mind.

The most notable occasion was when he was covering a royal inspection of the Fleet off Portsmouth. At one point, Brian told his listeners that the Queen had just left the deck and gone below. He went on to say, a moment later, that water was coming out of the side of the Royal yacht just above the water-line — which earned him a rebuke from his boss back in Portland Place.

He once spent the night in the Chamber of Horrors in Madame Tussaud's. The shaking in his voice was impressive, though possibly a touch exaggerated.

Another time, he lay in a hollow between the rails as the Golden Arrow steamed out from Victoria to Dover. I remember him devoutly hoping that no passenger would want to empty the pan onto the track as the train passed above his hide-out.

He was covering the funeral of George VI at Hyde Park Corner, when half-a-dozen mounted policemen came towards him through the arches of the gate, a trifle prematurely, as he thought.

'Here come', he said — with a note of surprise entering his voice — 'the police escort riding horses,' at which the producer of the programme back in Broadcasting House muttered into Brian's headphone 'What the devil did you think they would be riding — camels?'

Dear old Brian, always ready for a laugh — though on that occasion he suppressed it.

Later on in life, when Franklin Engleman died, Brian hosted 'Down Your Way' on radio for many years. Once he had clocked up the same number of programmes as his distinguished predecessor, he stood down — an unselfish gesture of the kind that Johnny Francome made some years later, when he gave up riding in races because he did not want to pass the record of a much-loved colleague who had had to give up riding after a bad fall.

I remember one 'Down Your Way' in which he interviewed an old man whose job had been to help John Snagge with his Boat Race commentary by riding his bicycle along the tow-path, keeping level with the two crews as he did so.

From this particular vantage point he would raise a light blue flag if Cambridge led and a dark blue one when Oxford was in the lead.

'You did this for a long time?' Brian asked.

'Ten years or more,' the old man told him.

'Wonderful,' said Brian, 'and I'm told you never made a mistake.'

'That's right,' said the old man.

'And how did you manage not to?' Brian asked.

'Quite easy,' said the old man, 'I just listened to that bugger John Snagge on the radio, that's how.'

The greatest claim to fame that Brian has, however, is the years that he has spent on 'Test Match Special' on the radio.

Though one of many well-known voices on the panel — such as 'Blowers', 'Truers' and 'the Alderman', to mention only three — the plain fact is that 'Johnners' holds his own among them without effort and, as a result, is better known now than he ever was before.

It could be that he talks more than his fellow-commentators. Also, possibly, the stories that he tells between times are more simple — and therefore more appealing — than those told by others. Possibly the kind of 'near-the-needle' *faux-pas* that he sometimes perpetrates enhances his popularity, as when he once remarked 'There's Compton in the gully with his legs wide apart waiting for a tickle.'

Then there are the cakes that his admirers send him. A year or two ago, a large sheet was hung on the gasometer that stands beside the Oval, on which was written in large letters 'Don't forget to give old Johnners his cakes' — demonstrating the great affection in which he is held.

Once or twice a week Brian addresses some dining-club or other, for which service he receives the sum of £1,500 or so, believe it or not. I am always telling him that he is over-paid — but that were he to ask, say, £2,000 for not making the speech the chances are that he would get it!

This is no doubt due to jealousy on my part, since I never have received remuneration for speech-making (nor indeed have I asked for it). Yet in Brian's case the strange thing is that, as one listens to all the same jokes that were made before the Flood and handed down by Noah and his crew to future generations, one can only conclude that the evening has been well worthwhile and that he deserves whatever his inspired and gifted agent can squeeze out of his admirers.

Never mind how old the jokes are or how often one has heard them before, the benignity and uninhibited delight with which he tells them charm his audience into submission long before he sits down, thus ensuring further invitations, further income and further benignity and uninhibited delight.

I have heard Brian say that his ambition in life was to be a stand-up comic. Some will argue that he always has been one, even though he does not function on the stage.

He operates in every other sphere, however, including the sick-room. Quite recently brother Alec found himself in hospital in Winchester. He spent more than three weeks in this splendid place, tended by first-class doctors and a very friendly nursing staff, some of whom may have been surprised to see on the shelf by his chair a row of what, in my youth, were called Brighton postcards — though the modern ones perhaps deserve a more descriptive phrase, as well as a health warning!

These doubtful postcards stood in full view of all his visitors, from ex-prime ministers to bishops, making Alec feel a great deal better every time he looked at them. I like to think he took them back to Scotland with him when he went home in good health.

The friendship between Alec and his postcard sender — Brian, needless to say — dates back more than fifty years. Two loves that they have always shared are cricket and Alec's late wife Elizabeth, according to the tale which I told earlier.

No friend of mine was ever closer to the family. If a doubtful story left his lips at mealtime when he was staying with us up in Scotland, he would look along the table at my father who may have looked faintly disapproving (though my mother never did!) and say, 'We understand each other, don't we, Lord Home' — thus releasing any tension in the atmosphere.

He is my youngest daughter Dinah's godfather. She got a letter from him on her twenty-first birthday enclosing a cheque for £99.99, with a little note attached which read, 'I'm very sorry, but I can't afford a hundred.'

Talk of godfathers reminds me that I am a godfather of Barry, Brian's eldest son. I remember his christening, which took place in the church just to the east of Lords, in an area which has always been the Johnston stamping-ground.

Some years later, his daughter Claire was married in the same church. Rachel, Jimmy Whatman and I sat in a pew together, after being given our service sheets by Brian, who was moving up and down the aisle greeting his friends.

The service started and we opened up our service sheets. To my amazement and to Jimmy's (Rachel's was not treated in the same way) we both found a picture of a very nubile naked lady stuck into our programmes opposite the first hymn.

I don't know how many other people in that congregation suffered the same treatment. What I do know is that Jimmy and I held our sheets very close to our chests.

'Vulgar', some would say — my mother would have said it definitely, even though she often laughed at Brian's less outrageous jokes.

The fact is that Brian's charm is such that it is quite impossible to take offence at anything that he may say or do. Nor does he pick and choose his audience. He treats a royal personage or someone equally exalted in the same way as he treats everybody else, regardless of their nationality, their background or their politics.

I rather think that he is a Conservative, although I've never questioned him on the point; he gives me the impression of being an honest right-wing character, just short of being a Blimp, who sees everybody else's point of view yet still regards his own as unimpeachable.

This does not mean that he is narrow-minded — only that he knows what suits him and sticks to it, while at the same time allowing the rest of us to follow our own stars.

His wife, Pauline, who has endured his jokes almost as long as I have, is a lady of great character, a loyal wife and mother who has given him five children, all of whom are very fond of him and laugh at all his jokes.

Barry is a broadcaster like his father. Andrew is a publisher, as is Ian. Claire has given Brian and Pauline some grandchildren. Among them is a grandson, and his proud grandfather tells me that he had his first net at Lords recently, as an eight-year-old.

The fact that Brian was not a first-class cricketer has never daunted him. He loves the game so much and all those who play it or have played it, that his cup is full to overflowing.

There was a time in our youth when he was faintly jealous of those who were in the first eleven at school. Indeed, I recall him saying once that Baerlein (the elder brother of the racing correspondent) stayed on at Eton until he was twenty-seven (with a wife and seven children) thus excluding Brian from the first eleven, of which Baerlein was the wicket-keeper. This, of course, was untrue, and Baerlein left Eton at precisely the same age as we did. But Brian delights in the thought of what, in his imagination, might have been.

There, then, is my estimate of Brian's character. If it seems superficial, it does so because I have deliberately concentrated on the lighter aspects of his life. This does not mean, however, that he has no serious side. On the contrary, the good deeds that he does are legion, including all the speeches that he makes for charity, which my informers tell me are as funny and as full as any that he makes on behalf of his bank manager.

He also puts in many personal appearances at functions dedicated to the welfare of groups of people — men, women or children — who are not so blessed with happiness as he has been throughout his life.

Nor are there many people who do not admire him. I have hardly ever heard him criticized except by his friends who like to bring him down as near as possible to earth.

I heard quite recently about some woman who saw fit to criticize him in public.

He told me of this himself when I rang up to tell him of my brother Alec's safe arrival in the land of his birth from the hospital in Winchester. He told me that he had been lunching at the BBC and had been placed next to the Queen Mother, which had thrilled him beyond measure. He was on a high when he left the building, only to be brought low a moment later when a female voice in the crowd shouted out 'Why don't you retire from "Test Match Special" and allow a younger man to take your place?'

'The bitch,' I say, without equivocation! Surely one of the things every woman knows (except for that misguided one) is that, like vintage port, he ought to be enjoyed in his old age and that it would be sacrilege were he to be replaced by some young fellow with a suitcase full of modern jokes. I told him this and I think it gave him some comfort.

Not everything I tell him does that! For example I often tell him that he ought to be knighted. 'What for?' he invariably asks.

'For services to insomnia,' I tell him, 'what with all those speeches you make and your incessant talking in "Test Match Special".'

Then he laughs, as he invariably does at any jokes against himself. Yet though I make a joke of it, I am also serious about it. I can think of nobody in any field of public life, in politics, sport, the City, the Commons, the services, business, local government, the world of entertainment or the board room who deserves an honour quite so much as Brian does (and has done for many years).

Since writing this, my friend has just been honoured with the CBE in the New Years Honours, much to my delight.

Good news, but roll on the day when a knighthood will be added to that well-earned accolade.

CHAPTER 14

S ince we moved to southern England from the Borders —
brought about by my dog sleeping on the piano top, the
reader may recall — we have made many friends in Hampshire.
Various relatives of Rachel's live — or, in some cases, lived —
there too, like Uncle Dick (he of the video that could not shake
off Sir John Betjeman's voice). And Grannie, Rachel's mother,
now in her ninety-first year, still lives at Mill Court, near Alton.

Mention of John Betjeman reminds me of a game of golf
I once played with Rachel and a friend called Christopher
Bridge, an inhabitant of Glynde in Sussex.

His wife, Dinah (Rachel's second cousin), had just had an
operation, so the four of us went to St Mawe's to stay in a
delightful hotel during her recuperation.

One night, after dinner, Christopher and Rachel and I
were planning a game of golf for the next day at St Enodoc.
Dinah suggested that we should get the hotel to make a sandwich
lunch for the next morning. She then called Elizabeth Cavendish,
Betjeman's faithful friend and companion, and expressed the hope
that the four of us would be welcome at John's house close to the
tenth (or was it the eleventh) hole. There we proposed to eat our
sandwiches before proceeding to the course, while Dinah took her
afternoon siesta in a deck-chair in the garden.

'Good idea,' Elizabeth said, 'we'd love to see you all.'

Off we went next morning; we arrived about one, took
a drink off John, and settled down to eat our sandwiches.

That done, we went towards the car to drive off to the
golf course, telling Dinah that we would return to pick her
up at the conclusion of the round.

As we turned to thank John and Elizabeth for entertaining
us, he said, 'How many of you are there playing?'

'Just the three of us,' we told him.

'I'd like to join you,' said he, much to our surprise.

We were surprised because he was no longer in his early
youth by any manner of means, nor were we aware that he

still played the game, although of course, we knew that he had once enjoyed it greatly, as witness his poem which had always been a favourite of mine, one verse of which — or part of one verse of which — runs as follows:

'I took an iron strong and true
And clipped it out of sight
And, spite of grassy banks between,
I knew I'd find it on the green.'

He told us he'd be with us in a jiffy (if I recollect the phrase correctly), and then he added, 'I'll get my clubs. They're in the car-port.'

He soon emerged with an old bag of very ancient clubs, not all of which appeared to be in prime condition.

'Some of them don't work too well,' he told us, 'but if I'm in trouble, I'm quite sure you'll lend me some of yours.'

'Of course,' we said in chorus.

Off we went, and on arrival at the club house, Christopher and I went on ahead to buy the green fees. When the man behind the counter asked for the full charge, we told him we were playing with a member.

'With which member?' he enquired politely.

'Sir John Betjeman,' we told him.

At that, both his eyebrows almost hit the ceiling. 'Sir John!' he said. 'He's not been on the course for ten or fifteen years.'

'Well, he will be this afternoon,' we said. At that moment, Rachel came in, followed by John. The official greeted him warmly, and made the necessary adjustment to our green fees on the spot.

We played about nine holes. Sir John, to start with, swung very slowly indeed, with the aim of simply hitting the ball, never mind how far it travelled. Whenever he decided to be a bit more ambitious, he asked one of us for the loan of a club.

'What a lovely club,' he said on one occasion, as he carefully addressed his ball with one of Christopher's woods and then swung and sent it on its way, both straight and true, though not very far.

When we reached the tenth (or the eleventh) hole, near his house, he excused himself and went home for his afternoon siesta, thanking us profusely for the game. We watched him on his way, then went on with our round, later returning to the house to pick up Dinah. By the time we got there, Dinah and Elizabeth had finished their siestas. When he had finished his, John joined us for a cup of tea and then proceeded to relive the holes that he had played, with relish and a deprecating smile. Afterwards we drove back towards St Mawe's, delighted with ourselves and at peace with all the world. Whenever I play there I think of John on the first tee and later on the fairway, loving every moment of the game that he had given up so many years before. I think, too, of the little church along the fairway of the tenth, above the green, in which John worshipped in his lifetime and where he lies buried now.

A splendid man was John, so kindly and so cultured, with a twinkle in his eye at all times. Also with a quite outstanding talent, which enabled him to write his poetry to such effect.

I was delighted to get a letter from John, praising a play of mine, *The Kingfisher*, that he had been to see and which he much enjoyed. I treasure it.

In memory of that delightful afternoon spent at St Enodoc, I penned a few lines which I sent off to Elizabeth and John.

> 'Ah, sandwiches in garden chairs.
> And daffodils and sun.
> And players splitting into pairs
> at twenty-five past one.
> Left-handed clergy on the tee.
> Sea air like ginger wine.
> John and my wife
> And Bridge and me.
> The first hole halved in nine.
> What matter while the sun stood high.
> And nobler far than that,
> swung somewhere between sea and sky
> a Poet Laureate.'

I remember that Elizabeth wrote me a letter to say that the Bard had thought kindly of my endeavour, although just how kindly she did not vouchsafe.

So much for Betjeman and Cornwall and St Enodoc. Now back to Hampshire, where we came to live in 1954.

We bought a house from Bobby Somerset, the father of Ann Rasch and David Somerset (now Duke of Beaufort), in the Meon Valley, for a sum of money which would scarcely buy a caravan these days. This was due not only to the market, but to Bobby's generosity as well.

The house was utterly enchanting, and we lived in it for more than thirty years.

The first new friend we found when we moved in was Mrs Cubitt, who lived a mile or two down the valley, at Hall Place, West Meon. She invited us to dinner soon after we moved in. From then on, we found her hospitality outstanding and her friendship stimulating.

Sonia Cubitt's mother was the well-known Mrs Keppel, the wife of Sir George Keppel and the mistress of Edward VII.

In a little volume that she wrote, I recollect a passage in which she remembered how her mother entered her nursery bedroom and said, 'Kingie's dead,' then kissed her goodnight in floods of tears.

Since rumour is the quite inevitable child of all romances, it is not surprising that one sometimes hears it said that Sonia was 'Kingie's' daughter. Other rumours bestow that distinction on her sister Violet Trefusis. Whether there is any truth in any of them, I am not in a position to judge. I only know that were I to ask Sonia's son, Harry Ashcombe, for his views on the matter he would merely smile and raise his eyebrows in loyal amusement.

Violet, Sonia's sister, was notorious in quite another way, through her relationship with Vita Sackville-West. We used to meet her at Hall Place, but we did not discuss her youthful peccadilloes.

I have a feeling that Sonia was rather in awe of her. Maybe I imagined it, but perhaps the memory of the embarrassment her sister caused her in her youth still lingered on.

As is well known — there having been a recent television programme on the subject — Vita Sackville-West loved Violet, with an uninhibited and violent passion, much to the dismay of their husbands, Denis Trefusis and Harold Nicolson. Nigel (Harold's son and Vita's) wrote a book about his mother and her female lover and then sold it for a television film.

According to some reports, he was unhappy with the way

the film turned out. My verdict, having watched most of it, was that it conveyed the atmosphere effectively, though perhaps the love scenes were a little overdone. Indeed, I wondered why the manager of the Paris hotel in which some of the most lurid episodes took place did not ask his guests to leave on the grounds that they made too much noise chasing one another round the foyer, through the lounge, up and down the stairs and in and out of bedrooms. But, now I come to think of it, I did not notice many other guests portrayed in the film. Perhaps they had already left, or the television company had taken over the hotel in its entirety.

I wrote a limerick on the affair for Sonia which pleased her greatly. It ran thus:

'Said Harold to Denis
At breakfast in Venice,
"Where's Violet — my Vita
Is longing to beat her."
"At tennis?" said Denis.'

So much for Sonia Cubitt, divorced wife of Roly Cubitt (later to become Lord Ashcombe), and a fascinating, friendly lady with a background of unending interest and a necessarily philosophical approach to life.

Another new friend we made was Bill Wightman, the oldest active racehorse trainer in the country. In those days, he was a great deal younger and in charge of a horse called Treetops Hotel, which was owned by Rachel's grandfather, Pop Hampden. Pop was then in his mid-eighties and lived at Mill Court with his eldest son and daughter-in-law, Leila, Rachel's mother.

Bill had been a prisoner-of-war of the Japanese. When he came home and he began his training again, he was somewhat thinner than he had been when he left at the beginning of the War, but just as keen.

We got to know him when we used to go with Pop to watch Treetops Hotel doing his early morning gallops. He won several nice races for his owner, which delighted Pop — still more so since he had never owned a racehorse before.

In later years, when I had had some theatrical successes which looked like keeping the bank manager at bay, this encouraged me to have a horse (two, on one occasion!) trained by Bill. One of them he bought me at the Ascot sales, and I named it Goblin. It won me seven races, and still holds the record over seven furlongs at Newmarket.

Nicknamed 'the wizard' in a racing column in *The Times* by Rachel's cousin, Michael Seeley, Bill loves the horses that he trains, regardless of their worth, and is an adept at winning good handicaps. I sometimes wonder whether he would rather win the Derby or a handicap on some north country course which he has had his eye on for some time, such is his satisfaction at manoeuvring a coup. By this I mean bringing the horse in question to its peak at the right time on the right day and at the right place.

Bill is quiet and sometimes rather cagey. He has a vintage sense of humour and a thoroughly forgiving nature, as was proved by his most recent reference to his Japanese imprisonment — a story which delights me every time I think of it.

He came out shooting in a Subaru a year or two ago. As I walked towards him, he wound down the window, grinning broadly.

'Bill,' I said, 'you told me many years ago that you would never, repeat never, till your dying day have anything around you that was Japanese.'

'I know I did,' said Bill.

'Then what', I asked him, 'are you doing in that Subaru?'

'I'll tell you,' he replied. 'I got a nomination to Mill Reef for someone in the City and he gave it to a business friend in Japan.'

'English or Japanese?' I enquired.

'Japanese,' said Bill.

'Go on,' I said.

'Well, he — the chap in Tokyo — sent me a present of £5,000.'

He opened the car door, and, as he got out, he said, 'I rather think that I misunderstood those people in the War.'

I told this story to my nephew, Andrew — my brother Edward's son — but suggested that he should not tell it to his father as it might upset him, as he too had been incarcerated by the Japanese.

'Don't worry, Uncle,' Andrew told me with a smile, 'he bought two yesterday.'

Another Hampshire friend is David Fraser, whom I have already mentioned. He and Julia, his wife, live happily in Islington, not far from Rachel's mother. I number him among my dearest friends and his wife is one of Rachel's dearest friends.

David comes from a military family from Aberdeenshire. His father and his grandfather were in the Grenadiers, and he has recently just published extracts from his father's diaries during two wars. His mother was the daughter of the famous actor, Cyril Maude, and his wife and co-star, Winifred Emery.

This gives to David's character a fascinating twist. At first glance, he could easily be labelled as a disciplined and, on occasion, somewhat straitlaced product of the Guards Brigade, but it is not difficult to catch sight of his more imaginative side.

A prime example of this dual outlook on life surfaced during dinner not long ago, when he addressed me thus.

'You've known me, William, ever since we met at Sandhurst at the beginning of the War.'

'Yes, General, I have indeed,' I told him, exercising my invariable habit of addressing him in military terms.

'Then you'll know the kind of politicians I admire, or otherwise,' he ventured.

'I've a shrewd idea about your likes and dislikes in all walks of life,' I told him.

'Right,' he said, 'then tell me who are the only politicians I've had reason to admire since the Gulf Crisis started.'

'Tony Benn and Ted Heath,' I suggested.

'Right,' he said, 'and right again.'

I did not have to ask why those two were considered worthy of his admiration. It was obvious that he favoured a policy towards Iraq less rigid than that adopted by the US President and his supporters.

To sum up his attitude — fairly, as I hope — I would say that he supports firm yet flexible politics and finds any kind of unconditional approach unconstructive and even disruptive in the long run.

This coming from a retired lieutenant-general, a vice-lieutenant of his county and a man whose nickname in the army was 'the razor', illustrates just how broad-minded — not to say surprising — he can sometimes be. It demonstrates that Fraser has a mind that is prepared not only to recognize the views of others, but to adopt them as well. Nor should such an attitude be taken to imply that he is inconsistent. On the contrary: it indicates a breadth of vision which I like to think is not all that unusual among military men.

Nor does such a point of view as the one he expressed that night mean that his strong loyalty to the military code of conduct is not still intact. Had he still been a serving soldier, and ordered to the Gulf, he would have carried out his orders even if he thought, deep down, that Tony Benn and Ted Heath were right in asking for a dialogue with Saddam Hussein, on the assumption that there might be common ground between the two sides once he had pulled out of Kuwait and that a war would solve few of the problems.

As far as military orders are concerned, David's attitude has always been that, never mind their contents, they must be obeyed.

This he made clear to me when we first met again, after the War, and clearer still when he appeared on television with me when a petition for my pardon from cashierment was being prepared.

Asked if he thought that I was right to disobey the order I was given at Le Havre, he answered 'Certainly not.' The way in which he emphasized each word caused some laughter in the studio, since many of those present knew that David was a friend of mine.

Then, quite unable to resist the merriment, in which I too had joined, David allowed his shoulders to start heaving rhythmically, *à la* Ted Heath, which added to the general hilarity.

Ah well, we all have different points of view — or rather some of us have different points of view from others — and the fact that David and I differ over the question of obeying orders does not mar our friendship in the least. Indeed, I like to think that he respects my wartime attitude, while at the same time wondering how anybody with a point of view like mine, so frequently and widely publicized, could possibly have been allowed to stay on in the army for so long, especially when I had asked to leave it.

David took to writing when he left the army, thus allowing his artistic genes to play a major role for the first time in his life. Since his retirement he has published a history of the British army, the life of Lord Alanbrooke, *Tales of Christine Watt* (stories of a Scotswoman of that name from Aberdeen) and many novels. The first group of these — a quintet — followed the lives of an English girl who had married a German officer before the War and her descendants.

He is now at work on a quartet of novels which follows the story of the Second World War through the eyes of an infantry regiment. The first volume, which was published recently, covers the period between the end of the 'phoney' war and the evacuation at Dunkirk. I find it fascinating. Every officer and soldier in the Westmorelands — as David has called his regiment — stands out in clear relief, and their characters are entirely credible. The final chapters, dealing with Dunkirk, leave one waiting impatiently for the second volume.

David was under-age when he arrived at Sandhurst in the first year of the War, so keen was he to join the army.

The army nearly lost him when a bomb dislodged the cistern in the lavatory that he was making use of at the time. Those of us who, only a few moments earlier, had sat round a table drinking coffee with him, thought that we had lost him, since — like some others, alas — he did not answer to the roll-call after the all-clear.

When he returned from hospital in Camberley a few days later, looking just the same as ever, he recounted to us his unhappy tale.

'You will recall', he told his friends as we sat round the coffee table once again, 'how we were sitting here that night when I got up to go and have a crap.'

'Yes, we remember, David,' we all chorused.

'Good. But what I'll bet you don't remember', said he, 'is that I had *The Times* crossword with me.'

'Yes, I do,' I told him, 'because I was hoping to get my hands on it.' Undeterred by this irrelevancy, David took the stage again.

'Then the bomb fell,' he told us, 'as you will all remember.' We nodded in unison. 'As a result of which, or to be accurate, as a result of its explosion,' he continued, 'I was knocked out by the cistern falling on my head.'

We sighed in sympathy (and in unison) and offered him another cup of coffee or another glass of port.

He raised his hand. 'I haven't finished yet,' he said. 'I came to in the hospital in Camberley at 0600 hours precisely the next morning and — and this is the important part — I had finished *The Times* crossword by the time they brought my breakfast an hour later.' At which we all drank his health.

I did not see him for the rest of the War, even though he was in Normandy at the same time as I was.

In his autobiography Peter Carrington tells of how he and David drove from Normandy to the newly-liberated Paris in a jeep, and of how, when they got lost in the suburbs, David saved the situation by directing their jeep-driver to the Ritz. When Peter asked him why he was so well-informed, he revealed that his father had been the military attaché at the British Embassy before the War.

Neither history nor David relates how many other sites they visited in Paris on that memorable outing, although Peter once informed me, when I put that very question to him, that he was a married man at that time. (For the reader's information, David was not.)

Frasers and Homes have had many happy holidays together with their children.

We pulled a fast one once on David when driving from Austria towards Aosta. We followed them through the frontier, and as we drove down into Italy we saw the Fraser car had put its hazard lights on and ground to a halt.

We pulled in behind, and David told us that he had mislaid his brief-case somewhere at the frontier post, and that they were going back to get it. In the meantime, he asked us to go on to a hotel in Aosta, where rooms had been booked in his name.

Wishing him the best of luck, we drove on to the hotel, where we were told that David's booking covered three or four small rooms for the children, plus two double bedrooms for the grown-ups.

The manager showed us into a drab double bedroom with a view of the main road.

'Could we see the other one?' Rachel asked.

'Certainly,' he said and took us down the corridor to a delightful double bedroom with a view over the mountains.

'This'll do for us,' we said together, as we dumped our suitcases and went off to deal with the children.

Half-an-hour or so later the Fraser caravan arrived. We were waiting by the front door of the hotel and, as the car drove up and David got out, we intoned the old slogan, 'You want the best rooms, we have them.'

To their eternal credit, all the Fraser family laughed.

On another trip from Paris to the Ile de Ré, off La Rochelle, the General imbibed, as I recall, a little too much red wine during the lunch break. This had a mildly adverse effect on his stomach just as we arrived outside the house that we had rented for the holiday.

The General walked hurriedly towards the house, but could not find the front door key.

He did not linger long, however, but doubled back to where we had left the cars.

When I returned to unload our car half a minute later, having found the key under the mat, I found David in a nearby hollow digging a latrine.

'It's all right, we've got in,' I told him — but he paid no attention, so fascinated was he by a task he found himself performing for the first time since the early stages of the War.

I left him digging and when I returned towards the house a minute or two later with some of our luggage, I was pleased to see him putting the result of his hard labour to good use.

A Hampshire lady who befriended us was Esmé Rhyl. Her husband Nigel Birch — as he was known before he got his peerage — was a proper character. He was one of the trio — Enoch Powell and Lord Thorneycroft were the two others — who provided Uncle Harold with his 'little local difficulty'.

Nigel had a sharp tongue and a razor-clear brain — and a life-saving sense of humour.

In the hall of his house, there still hangs a picture which he commissioned of Harold Macmillan in a Chinese costume, squatting on the floor of some Chinese abode. Underneath it is written, in Chinese, 'You never had it so good'.

There is an avenue in front of his house, at the far end of which — or so he liked to say — he planned to erect a statue of Macmillan, so much did he have him on his mind. He died before he had time to achieve that ambition.

I was never privileged to see the two of them together but I am ready to believe that such a meeting would have been conducted, had it taken place after their political parting of the ways, in an atmosphere of mutual respect.

Others in our orbit are Mark Wyndham and his second wife, Patricia, who have come to live near Froxfield. Mark is the younger brother of John Wyndham, who was Uncle Harold's right hand man throughout the War years. He was an amusing, friendly and delightful fellow and a great wit.

On one occasion, John had a friend to stay for the weekend at Petworth. Like Queen Mary he suffered an uncontrollable urge to get his hands on any ornament — never mind its value — that caught his fancy as he strolled around the house.

On the Monday morning, John was waiting in the hall for his friend to leave, and as he came down the stairs, John called out to him, 'Your taxi's here, to take you to the station.' And he added, 'Customs will be in the hall.'

What a kindly, eccentric, friendly fellow John was. So too — now I consider it — is his younger brother Mark. (I trust that final tribute will mean some good dinners in the future.)

These and other friends we got to know when we were living in the Meon Valley, in the house that Bobby Somerset had sold me for a song. We then moved five or six miles west to Kilmeston.

I mean to cover that in my next (and last) chapter, in which I will describe our traumatic journey from an old house we had loved for more than thirty years into a new one built in 1967, of which our youngest daughter remarked, the first time she came through the front door, 'This is the first house I've been in that is younger than me.'

CHAPTER 15

'Why did you leave that lovely house?' I'm always being asked.

I'm then reminded yet again that it was the perfect place in which to live, looking across the Meon Valley from its lovely garden made by Betty Somerset. Such enquiries always end with the phrase 'I'll never understand why you and Rachel left it. It was perfect for you!' As, indeed, it was.

But, nonetheless, we had to leave it for financial reasons, as I always explain patiently to my inquisitors.

'That's what you say,' they argue, 'but the fact is that you sold a house with three and a half acres and then bought one with just over twenty acres.'

'That's right,' I say, 'and I sold a seven-acre field the moment that I got to Derry House, and now we've got thirteen exactly.'

'Which is nearly five times more than you had in the other place,' they say.

'That's right,' I tell them, 'but I got a lot of money for it: considering that Bobby Somerset had kindly sold it to me in 1955 for £10,000 or thereabouts, I didn't do too badly.'

'How much did you get for it?' they ask, displaying all the candid curiosity which is the hallmark of one's friends.

'That's my affair,' I say. 'But it was a great deal of money. In fact in a long life I have never made a sum of money like that — not through *The Reluctant Debutante* or any other play or film. Anyway,' I continue, 'the house has only got five bedrooms, whereas Drayton had eight, and it's only twenty-seven years old.'

Thus the conversation goes when I am cross-questioned by people who assume that a successful playwright must be rich.

The fact is, of course, that a playwright is rich for as

long as a successful play continues to bring in the necessary income. After that, unless his next play proves equally successful, he will start to feel the pinch, especially if he is lacking any private means of his own.

That is the situation that prevails in my set-up. For nearly fifty years, I was comparatively comfortable financially, relying almost entirely on what I made from my play-writing — apart from the small sum I inherited, which very soon ran out.

This 'small sum' consisted of £12,000 — which was quite a nest egg when I started life but soon dwindled down to nothing in the post-war years.

So when the shoe began to pinch in the late Seventies and Eighties, as a result of having no successful plays on, Rachel and I found ourselves afloat upon a sea of ever-growing debt. After consulting lawyers and friends, we decided that we could not carry on unless we sold our house.

We came to this decision with profound regret. Rachel was broken-hearted, since Drayton House had been for thirty years her dream house, the home in which she had brought up all her children, seen them through their schooling and then launched them on the world.

And for me it was a sorrow too, of course: but men are more resilient than women when it comes to property — except perhaps for those who live in their ancestral homes, which have been handed down for generations. Both of us became ill as a result of having to sell our beauty spot.

After the sale had been arranged, we went to stay with Rachel's mother while our new home was being refurbished. Rachel had a breakdown there and was ill for some months. Not to be outdone, I was taken ill with what was diagnosed as a slow heart.

One afternoon Rachel and I went to see a doctor in Liss, near my mother-in-law's home. He told me that my heart was not functioning quite as it should. An ambulance took me to the King Edward VII Hospital at Midhurst, Rachel following in the car. As soon as we arrived there, Dr Gabe, whom I took to at once, arranged for me to be taken to London some days later in another ambulance. Rachel continued to look after me, although she was unwell herself. At the Middlesex Hospital I was examined by Dr

Swanton, who told me he was going to fit me with a pace-maker. Much to my surprise the operation took only twenty minutes to perform, under a local anaesthetic.

I left the Middlesex a few days later. As I shook hands with Dr Swanton, he said, 'Now you've had the operation, you'll find you can do things a lot better than you have in recent years.'

'Does that include golf?' I enquired facetiously.

'What was your handicap?' he asked me.

'Twenty-four, when I last took it out,' I told him.

He smiled. 'Sorry,' he said, 'I can't promise much advance there!'

Nonetheless, there has been some improvement, as I told him when we next met.

I returned to Midhurst to convalesce. Rachel came to see me every day and Dr Gabe made her stay the night on one occasion, as she was unwell.

Some ten days later, Rachel drove me to our new home. I found that she had been working non-stop to get the house ready so as to make sure that my home-coming was as happy as it could be — which indeed it was.

Downstairs, our pictures had all been hung in impeccable taste by Mark Wyndham, leaving me to do the upstairs bedrooms while I was recuperating. Family and friends all rallied round, and in a few months Rachel was well enough to start a garden in a field which had, till then, held horses, since Derry had been a stud farm. One sunny summer day, I followed Rachel in my Toro tractor as she walked in front of me, planning where to put the garden paths. So sound was her judgement that we have never had occasion to change them since, though occasionally we have added to them.

Now the garden she created is beginning to establish itself. In another year or so, it will begin to look as though it has been there for quite some time, even though it was, in fact, a bare field until the mid-1980s.

During that time, we have come to love both the house and its garden — which is tended tenderly twice a week by David Bradley, a green-fingered neighbour in the village. Although we never, for one moment, imagined that such a thing would ever happen when we first rebuilt our nest, we are as happy here as we were in the past — and so are all our children, when they come to visit us.

We pray that we will never have to move house again, although the prospect of it sometimes looms in more depressing moments — when we have 'flu, for example.

We do everything we can to keep this prospect at bay and live in the hope that, should there be another crisis in our lives, we will surmount it. Even so, the prospect of my old age being spent without sufficient means is ever present unless things change a great deal for the better.

Meanwhile, I am writing this book and preparing to write a new play — not to mention my domestic tasks. These were summed up by my daughter Dinah when replying to a question put to her by Harry Marriott — then her fiancé, now her husband.

'Does your father still write plays?' I heard him ask her as they were sitting together on the sofa in the library.

'No, he can't,' she said, 'because he's always laying the table!'

'Am I finished,' I sometimes ask myself, 'or am I merely out of fashion?'

The answer, as I see it, is 'Not finished, no, but out of fashion, yes — a hundred times, yes.'

If I was finished, there would be no sign of popularity whatever. People would not read my plays here or in any other country, nor would they be performed by amateurs, touring companies and repertories (including, I hope, a revival of one of my more successful plays in Paris next year).

Nor would the press cuttings I get, reporting amateur and local productions of my plays up and down the country, read quite so consistently well. All this convinces me that I am only temporarily out of fashion, rather than a spent force which has no chance of returning to its former strength.

And even if, through old age or force of circumstances or both, I were to give up writing plays, there is little danger of inaction setting in, or lack of interest leading me to lose my zest for life: my days would still be full!

For example, I may spend the morning in walking to

the bus stop for the papers and then, once I have brought the logs in from outside the back door, writing letters. Around midday, I will lay and light the fire in the sitting-room and the stove in the library, sit myself down with a gin and tonic or, on Sunday a bloody Mary; after which I will get down to *The Times* crossword, followed by the other daily paper crosswords.

Around one, I call to Rachel through the kitchen door, 'How many courses and how many customers?' The answer having been received, I lay the table in the library, which doubles up as a dining-room. That done, I turn on the one o'clock news. If this proves unexciting I resume the crossword and my gin and tonic until lunch is served by Rachel, my most admirable cook.

The meal concluded, I pick up the dirty glasses and the empty plates, go through into the kitchen with them, and insert them in the washing-up machine, at the same time restraining Jack, our pug, from licking all the dirty knives and forks. That work concluded, and while Rachel is still tidying the kitchen, I embark on my siesta, billed to last an hour but sometimes cut short by a racing programme on the television or a game of golf with Rachel.

After tea — which I do not imbibe — I give the dogs (Tinker, my daughter Dinah's spaniel, and Jack Pug) their evening meal, eject them through the door, put any dirty tea-cups in the washing-up machine, and let the dogs in again.

At around six-thirty, I pour my first whisky (water with no ice) and continue with the crossword. I then go up to run the bath, where Rachel joins me after laying the foundations of our dinner in the kitchen.

Down again, after the bath, with my instructions received for laying the table and for placement, I resume work on the crosswords or, if they are finished, carry on reading some enjoyable book.

Our dinner over, while the guests — if there are any — go into the sitting-room for coffee I remain behind to clear the table, brushing whatever crumbs there are onto the floor for Jack, and refill and switch on the washing-up machine.

And so to bed — quite early when we have no guests, some time later (on occasion much, much later) when we have a lot of talkative and merry people dining with us.

That, then, is the story of my life to date. Anyone who thinks that, although I have reached retirement age, I am no longer working should think again — and perhaps concede that I lead a very full and happy life about which I have no complaints whatever, blessed as I am with a washing-up machine, a nice house and a perfect wife.

INDEX